CONVENT OF LAS DESCALZAS REALES. MADRID

Areas open to the public
(*areas closed to the public)

GROUND FLOOR
1 Vestibule. Ticket office. Shop-bookshop
2 Nuns' Lobby
3 Lower Cloister
4 Main staircase

FIRST FLOOR
4 Main staircase
5 Upper Cloister (5 to 28)
WEST GALLERY OF THE UPPER CLOISTER
6 Chapel of the Recumbent Christ
7 St Joseph's Chapel
8 Chapel of *El Peñasco*
9 Chapel of Our Lady of the Rosary
10 St Michael's Chapel
SOUTH GALLERY OF THE UPPER CLOISTER
11 Chapel of the Annunciation
12 Sacristy display cabinet
13 St Agnes's Chapel
14 Organist's glass case
15 Antechoir (15 to 18)
16 Chapel of Our Lady of El Puig
17 Chapel of Our Lady of Peace
18 St Anthony's Chapel
19 Choir
EAST GALLERY OF THE UPPER CLOISTER
20 Chapel of the Immaculate Conception
21 Chapel of Our Lady of Guadalupe
22 Chapel of St Francis of Paola
23 Chapel of Our Lady of the Angels
24 Ecce Home Chapel
NORTH GALLERY OF THE UPPER CLOISTER
25 Girls' Showcase
26 Guardian Angel Chapel
27 Chapel of Our Lady of Montaigu
28 Chapel of Our Lady of Refuge
29 Staircase of the Redeemer

SECOND FLOOR
29 Staircase of the Redeemer
30 Tapestry Room
31 Chapel of the Dormition *
32 Holy House of Nazareth *
33 Chapel of the Miracle *

MEZZANINE
34 Room of the Guardian Angel
35 Chapel of the Guardian Angel
36 Cell of the Infanta Margarita
37 "Candilón"
38 Chapter House
39 Hall of the Kings
40 Relics Chapel *
41 Oratory corridor
42 Oratory
43 Flemish Room corridor
44 Flemish Painting Room
45 Room of Spanish and Italian Painting

46 CHURCH. GROUND FLOOR (46 to 51)
    (open during hours of worship)
47 Chapel of St John the Baptist
48 St Sebastian's Chapel
49 Presbytery
50 Nuns' communion rail *
51 Tomb of the founder,
    Doña Juana of Austria

AROUND THE CONVENT
A Calle de la Misericordia.
    Plaza de Las Descalzas
B Calle Postigo de San Martín

THE CONVENTS OF LAS DESCALZAS REALES AND LA ENCARNACIÓN

ANA GARCÍA SANZ
Mª LETICIA SÁNCHEZ HERNÁNDEZ

REALES SITIOS DE ESPAÑA

© PATRIMONIO NACIONAL, 2003
Palacio Real de Madrid
Bailén, s/n
28071 Madrid
Tel. 91 547 53 50

© Texts:
Ana García Sanz
(The Convent of Las Descalzas Reales)
Mª Leticia Sánchez Hernández
(The Convent of La Encarnación)

© Photographs:
Patrimonio Nacional - Félix Lorrio - Antonio Úbeda
Aldeasa - José Barea

N.I.P.O.: 006-03-013-6
I.S.B.N.: 84-7120-343-X
National book catalogue number: M-43673-2003

Co-ordination and production:: ALDEASA
Design and layout: Myriam López Consalvi
Translation: Jenny Dodman
Photograph setting: Lucam
Printed: Estudios Gráficos Europeos. S.A.

Cover photograph: Convent of Las Descalzas,
detail of church facade.

Back cover photograph: Convent of La Encarnación,
detail of main facade.

Printed in Spain

Table of contents

Foreword

PATRIMONIO NACIONAL is the institution which administers the State properties in the service of the Crown by performing the representative functions assigned to it by the Spanish Constitution and Spanish law.

These properties comprise a number of palaces, monasteries and convents founded by monarchs, which are of great historic, artistic and cultural importance; most significantly, they are of outstanding *symbolic value*. The Royal Palaces of Madrid, El Pardo, Aranjuez, San Ildefonso and La Almudaina continue to be used for the residential and representative purposes for which they were built centuries ago. In these buildings His Majesty the King carries out his duties as Head of State – particularly in the Royal Palace of Madrid, which is the official royal residence and, as such, the highest embodiment of this *symbolic value*.

In addition to these functions, Patrimonio Nacional has a specific cultural duty consisting of making the buildings and other possessions available for study and research and visits by the public.

Both the buildings and the Spanish Royal Collections (comprising 27 different categories ranging from fans to tools and including silverware, painting, tapestries, furniture, musical instruments and clocks, etc.) are distinguished by the very characteristics that make Patrimonio Nacional a unique cultural institution. These are: *their particular purpose*, since they are still used by the Spanish royal family; their *historical authenticity*, as the items were once commissioned, acquired or presented as gifts for the buildings that house them; their *originality*, given the absence of replicas or imitations; and their extraordinary *artistic, historic and symbolic value*. The visitor will therefore appreciate that Patrimonio Nacional is much more than just a museum.

The Spanish Royal Palaces are surrounded by green spaces that currently span approximately 20,500 hectares. Gardens and parkland account for some 500 and the remaining 20,000 is woodland (parts of which are open to the public) belonging to El Pardo, La Herrera and Riofrío. These areas, mainly of the Mediterranean forest biotype, are of great ecological importance and provide a worthy setting for the monuments they surround.

Since their foundation, the Royal Monasteries and Convents have been served by the same religious orders, except for San Lorenzo de El Escorial, which passed from the Hieronymites to the Augustinians as a result of disentailment in the 19th century. They enjoy special importance in Spanish history, as they owe their establishment to the personal patronage of the monarchs.

In addition to serving a cultural purpose, the tours organised for the general public attempt to make Spanish visitors more fully aware of the symbolic value of these places, so that they may identify with them and feel they are heirs to Patrimonio Nacional's immense historical and artistic treasures.

The influence of these treasures, acquired by the Spanish Crown over the centuries, on Spain's cultural identity has been, and continues to be, decisive.

The "Patronatos Reales"

THE TERM *patronato* has various meanings: it refers to the right or power exercised by a person – the patron – over a foundation, generally religious, and his or her duty to fulfil certain related obligations, and also denotes the link established between the patron and his or her works. *Patronato Real* has two meanings in Spanish: it can refer either to the universal patronage exercised by the Spanish monarchs vis-à-vis the Spanish Church, including the right to propose candidates for ecclesiastical posts, or to the special link between the monarchs and the foundations they established.

As patrons of all the churches in the country, monarchs could be patrons of any chapel, monastery, convent, hospital or charitable institution. They could also engage in personal patronage by making endowments to religious institutions, as provided in Canon Law. They could do so in several ways: as heads of state, with the public treasury at their disposal; as heads of the royal household, using royal funds to link the institution to the household; or personally, using their own money to establish a church or monastery. These distinctions are essentially abstract and therefore difficult to separate in practical terms, as on many occasions religious institutions came under royal patronage through royal decree. Therefore, while some foundations were indeed established using the money of the monarchs or of the royal household, others were merely awarded the honorific status of royally protected institutions, entitling monarchs to enjoy privileged sites or to place the royal arms in prominent places. When the monarchs were granted universal patronage of the Spanish Church, almost all the places of worship and religious houses came under the protection of the crown, and the Chamber of Castile began to compile an alphabetical register of all the religious foundations under the patronage of the kings and queens.

The two foundations described in this guidebook, Las Descalzas Reales and La Encarnación in Madrid, can be said to be *Patronatos Reales*, since they enjoy the protection of the Spanish monarchs and have a number of obligations towards the Spanish royal household, whose duty it is to finance the buildings and maintain the communities who live there. The charters of foundation issued by the patrons – Princess Juana of Portugal in the case of Las Descalzas Reales and Philip III for La Encarnación – constitute what are known as the "foundation responsibilities", as they lay down provisions governing each and every aspect of the running of the foundations. These include: rights and duties of the nuns; the role of the chaplains and ministers; the financial endowment made to the institution; and the material needs of the building.

The term "to found" relates both to the construction of a building and to the establishment of any kind of institution designed for a specific purpose. These concepts may be separate or may coincide, as in the case of the two convents in question, which are institutions established in buildings designed specifically for that purpose. The institutions are: the Order of the Poor Clares, who live in what was once the palace of the royal bookkeeper Alonso Gutiérrez and is now Las Descalzas Reales; and the Order of the Augustinian Nuns who live in the building erected by Juan Gómez de Mora, today the Convent of La Encarnación, which stands opposite what used to be the Colegio de Doña María de Aragón (now the Senate).

In the 17th century foundations were the responsibility of the ecclesiastical authorities, according to a general law which had long been in force. The Church recognised the right of any person to use all or part of his or her possessions to perform charitable works, which could be carried out either directly by the benefactor or through an intermediary, depending on the terms and duration of the aims pursued. If the benefactors wished their endowment to be perpetual, as in the case of Royal Patrons, they asked the Church to raise it to the status of legal entity and sought a permanent body capable of fulfilling the aims stipulated in the foundation charter. A foundation is therefore a monetary donation raised to the status of legal entity.

The Convents of Las Descalzas Reales and La Encarnación in Madrid were established by means of donations (the endowment included the buildings, sums of money and art and everyday objects) made by their founders – Juana of Austria and Philip III – and their successors (who also became the foundations' patrons). As a result the ownership of these assets passed from the founders to the foundations (the *Patronatos*). The founders appointed administrators (currently Patrimonio Nacional) to perform the so-called foundation responsibilities – in this case, perpetual prayer for the patrons and their successors – while the promoters enjoyed certain privileges at the *Patronato*: private visits, special prayers, burials, supervision of the admission of nuns, etc.

The establishment of foundations by the Spanish monarchs was governed by the regulations laid down by the Council of Trent and authorised by means of specific papal bulls and briefs on the performance of specific actions and solemn liturgical ceremonies; for this reason the foundations, all of which are religious in nature, were given the name of *Patronatos Reales* and the monarchs became their Royal Patrons.

The most important *Patronatos Reales* established throughout the history of Spain and still linked to the crown under the administration of Patrimonio Nacional are: Santa María la Real de Las Huelgas in Burgos, founded by Alfonso VIII and Eleanor of England in 1187; Santa María la Real in Tordesillas, built by Peter I *the Cruel* in 1363; San Lorenzo el Real at the Escorial, built by Philip II in 1563; and Santa Isabel in Madrid, established by Blessed Alonso de Orozco.

The Convent of Santa Isabel, whose full name is La Visitación de Nuestra Señora, was established in 1589 by Philip II's preacher, Alonso de Orozco, for the cloistered Augustinian nuns belonging to the reform he carried out within the Augustinian Order. The endowment was made by Prudencia Grillo, a famous Madrid widow who became a nun at Orozco's convent together with her three maids. The first community lived in houses belonging to the widow on Calle del Príncipe near the old playhouse of the same name. The deaths of the founder and benefactress plunged the community into a serious financial crisis, which, together with the bad state of repair of the building and the noise from the theatre, prompted the nuns to ask Margaret of Austria for royal patronage. The queen agreed, albeit on two conditions: that the nuns adopt the Augustinian Rule of Mariana de San José and Agustín Antolínez, and that they move to Calle Santa Isabel – where they currently live – to the former palace of Antonio Pérez, whose possessions had been confiscated by the crown. The move took place in 1610.

The two foundations in question, Las Descalzas Reales and La Encarnación, are an embodiment both of the Spanish monarchs' service to the Roman Catholic Church and of their desire to keep their memory and that of their successors perpetually alive.

Mª Leticia Sánchez Hernández

THE CONVENT OF
LAS DESCALZAS REALES

Introduction

IN CLOSE proximity to the Convent of San Martín, which gave its name to the outlying district where it was located, stood a palace as early as the 15th century. By the beginning of the 16th century it had passed into the hands of Don Alonso Gutiérrez, bookkeeper to Emperor Charles V. The building, which was subsequently converted into a convent dedicated to Our Lady of Solace, has housed a community of Poor Clares, popularly known as the Descalzas Reales or Royal Discalced Nuns, since 1559.

This name stems from the simple sandals the Clares wore all year round and the fact that the convent was a royal foundation. It was Juana of Austria, Charles V's youngest daughter, who established the convent. After being widowed by Prince John, heir to the Portuguese throne, she returned to Castile and was summoned by her father to act as regent of the Spanish kingdoms in Valladolid, as Prince Philip was to depart for England. Despite leaving her four-month old son Sebastian behind in Lisbon, Juana never returned to Portugal. After being released from her duties to the state, she concentrated on founding a religious and social complex. Juana's project comprised buildings with different functions: a convent for prayer and shelter; a royal residence; a charity hospital; a school for orphaned girls; and the necessary outbuildings and areas to ensure self-sufficiency, such as vegetable gardens, dairies and a bakery.

Her intention was to create a convent inhabited by a female branch of the Society of Jesus and, with this aim in mind, she conferred with Francisco de Borja, general of the Society. However, she finally decided to establish a new community of Franciscan nuns comprising seven sisters from the Convent of Santa Clara in Gandía.

The choice of the building which was to house the new community was partly due to sentimental reasons. In 1535, Empress Isabella of Portugal stayed at Alonso Gutiérrez's palace to give birth to Juana, her youngest daughter, on 23 June. Years later, in 1555, the infanta purchased the building from Don Alonso's heirs and entrusted the architect Antonio Sillero with the task of restructuring the palace to adapt it to its new role as a convent. The works began in 1556 and were still incomplete when the first community of nuns arrived at the convent in 1559.

The alterations also included the construction of a church in 1564; however, Juana died prematurely in September 1573 and did not see the complex completed.

The convent's doors remained closed to the public for centuries. In 1960 the board of trustees of Patrimonio Nacional, with the consent of the Franciscan nuns, decided to open the main areas to the general public. After papal authorisation was granted to suspend the rules of enclosure at certain times of day and the necessary formalities were completed, the Convent of Las Descalzas Reales was opened to the public on 1 December 1960.

Since then the public has enjoyed the privilege of visiting an inhabited, living space where the works of art convey both the essence

Entrance to the convent.

Its current patron is His Majesty King Juan Carlos I, whose duties in this respect are performed through Patrimonio Nacional.

On 18 February 1994 it was declared an "Asset of Cultural Interest" and accorded the status of "Monument" by means of a Royal Decree.

The tour

Ground floor

The vestibule and the Nuns' Lobby

The entrance to the convent is a Renaissance-style door leading to the vestibule, where a display cabinet contains a painting of *Our Lady of Solace*, to whose protection the convent's first nuns entrusted themselves.

A wooden door decorated with medallions leads into the Nuns' Lobby, which is decorated with six paintings by Bartolomé Román, a 17th-century artist. They depict five of the seven archangels – *Gabriel, Michael, Raphael, Zadkiel* and *Barachiel* – and the *Guardian Angel*. The four bronze candlesticks were made by an anonymous 16th-century Flemish artist and belonged to the tomb of Empress Maria of Austria.

The Lower Cloister

The central courtyard of what was originally the palace was converted into the convent's cloister. Weather conditions, which had begun to affect both the nuns' health and the works of art, prompted the community to ask for it to be walled off. The architect Francisco Sabatini supervised the works in 1773, as is stated in an inscription on the west wall of the cloister.

The capitals of the original palace colonnade were discovered and the groups

of convent life and the role of the *Patronato Real* over the centuries. The provenance of these works varies; whether part of the nuns' dowries, acquired through successive donations or commissioned expressly for the community, all of them have progressively enriched the rooms of this convent.

Since the building was opened as a museum, constant cataloguing, research and restoration work has been carried out, particularly in 1985 and 1986. These efforts were taken into consideration by the European Museum of the Year Prize Committee when it awarded the convent the Council of Europe's Museum Prize in 1987. In 2002 the Tapestry Room underwent a complete architectural restoration to provide new museum space. In 1999, interesting architectural remains of the former palace and the early decoration of the convent were discovered.

The Convent of Las Descalzas Reales is a foundation under the patronage of the crown.

14

▲ *Alonso Sánchez Coello:* Juana of Austria. *Candilón.*

◄ *General view of the main facade.*

Top, Bartolomé Román: The Archangel St Raphael *(left) and* The Guardian Angel *(right). Nuns' Lobby.* ▲

Below, view of the Lower Cloister.

of three columns at the corners of the cloister were recovered during the course of recent architectural restoration work.

Four paintings executed by Diego de Urbina between 1573 and 1586 decorate the cloister's altars. They depict *Glory*, *The Holy Family*, *The Prayer in the Garden* and *The Adoration of the Shepherds*. There is also a set of canvases representing scenes of hermits. These were painted by the Flemish school and are copies of a number of engravings, housed in the convent, made by Jan and Raphael Sadeler after drawings by Marten de Vos.

On the north wing hang the portraits of: *Maria Luisa Gabriela of Savoy*, which was produced by the studio of Miguel Jacinto Meléndez and dates from the early 18th century; *Charles III* as king of Naples, a Neapolitan work displaying the influence of Giuseppe Bonito and dated to c. 1740; and lastly, a 17th-century *Allegory of Vanity*.

The main staircase

The magnificent staircase consisting of two flights of stairs with a large landing was originally the principal palace staircase. It was built in the early 16th century, though the pictorial decoration mostly dates from the 17th century. The walls of the impressive stairwell are totally covered in mural paintings depicting religious themes, the oldest being the trompe l'oeil paintings representing cloisters and gardens with altars and statues. Amid the mock architectural

▲ *Main staircase. View from the landing, showing the* Archangels *and* The Calvary.

Main staircase. View of approach to the Upper Cloister, showing the Royal Balcony of Philip IV's family on the wall. ▶

The *Opening of the Heavens* decorating the ceiling and some of the architectural themes are attributed to Claudio Coello.

Between the two entrance archways to the upper cloister is the following inscription: RESTAVRO ESTA ESCALERA SOR ANA DOROTEA MARQVESA DE AVSTRIA HIJA DEL EMPERADOR RODOLFO II RELIGIOSA DE ESTE CONVENTO AÑO 1684 (This staircase was restored by Sister Ana Dorotea Marchioness of Austria, daughter of Emperor Rudolf II and nun of this convent, in the year 1684). This is the first mention of Sister Ana Dorotea, a nun who promoted many artistic projects at the convent.

The paintings decorating the stairway also include the busts of *St Francis*, *St Clare* and *St Dorothy* and representations of *Hope*, *Faith*, *Charity* and *Religion*.

First floor

The Upper Cloister. West and south wings

The conversion of the upper gallery of the courtyard into a cloister led to the establishment of many chapels in areas formerly used as palace rooms. In this part of the cloister there are seven chapels and a number of glass cases containing various devotional images.

The first chapel is dedicated to the worship of the image of the *Recumbent Christ*, an expressive 16th-century polychrome wood carving attributed traditionally to the Andalusian artist Gaspar Becerra. A special privilege dating back to the establishment of the convent allows this image to be carried in a procession held on the afternoon of Good Friday, displaying the Blessed Sacrament in a recess in its chest.

A notable feature of the *St Joseph's Chapel* is a 17th-century Spanish image of the saint.

structures and reliefs are *The Seven Archangels* accompanied by *The Guardian Angel* and *The Guardian Angel of the Community*. Although there is no record of who painted them, they may be the work of Ximénez Donoso and Matías de Torres.

The group of paintings depicting the *Calvary* are located in a prominent place and exalt the Passion of Christ in connection with the establishment of the Eucharist. Opposite this scene is the *Royal Balcony*, where the members of the royal family are portrayed – Philip IV, his second wife Mariana of Austria, the Infanta Margarita Teresa and the then Prince of Asturias, Felipe Próspero. Both paintings are attributed to Antonio de Pereda and are dated earlier than 1661, the year that the young infante who appears in the painting died at the age of four.

▲ *Gaspar Becerra:* Recumbent Christ. *Upper Cloister.*

Although the walls are decorated with many small devotional paintings, the most outstanding features of this chapel are the polychrome wooden ceiling and frieze displaying the coat of arms of Alonso Gutiérrez. This ceiling formerly belonged to one of the palace rooms and owes its survival to the fact that it was concealed and protected by another one built during a later period. Equally interesting is the dado of Talavera tiles which, like others found in the convent, may be part of the original palace decoration.

The *Chapel of El Peñasco* houses a large *Christ on the Cross*, an anonymous early 17th-century work. The chapel is named after the altar in the shape of a hill or *peñasco*. It contains images of a number of Franciscan saints – *St Francis*, *St Anthony*, *St Peter of*

Alcántara and *St James of Alcalá* – and small caves with sculptures of hermit saints.

A salient feature of this area of the cloister is the painting of *Our Lady of Begoña*, a votive offering for a miracle worked by this image. The painting was executed by Francisco de Mendieta in 1588.

The *Chapel of Our Lady of the Rosary*, also known as the *Sweet Name of Jesus*, displays a large painting of *The Glorification of the Christ Child* by the 17th-century Madrid school. The image of the Our Lady of the Rosary, after whom the chapel is named, stands in a side niche. Also of interest is the *Christ Child with Instruments of the Passion* on the main altar, a sculpture by Pedro de Mena's circle.

The *Holy Family Protected by St Michael* hangs in a prominent position in *St Michael's Chapel*. This large canvas is a 17th-century

View of the Upper Cloister, south wing. ▲

nun, since she lived as a Clare after being widowed. She is shown receiving communion from Archduke Charles, her husband, depicted as St Charles Borromeo. Nine of the couple's children witness the scene; their names are shown on the back of the canvas. This painting, in which people are used as models for saints, is attributed to Juan Pantoja de la Cruz.

We next come to the *Chapel of the Annunciation*, which was built expressly to house the *Annunciation* Fra Angelico painted for the Convent of San Domenico in Fiesole between 1430 and 1435. This painting was a gift to the convent in 1611 from the Duke of Lerma. In the 19th century it was transferred to the Prado, where it currently hangs, on the wishes of Francisco de Asís, the king consort. It was replaced by an *Annunciation* attributed to Luis de Madrazo, who drew his inspiration from the one by Allori at the church of the Annunziata in Florence. Around the chapel are remains of the mural painting that originally decorated this wall of the cloister before the arrival of Fra Angelico's picture.

The paintings of *St James*, *The Saviour* and *St Lorenzo* may have been executed by Bartolomé Carducho at the beginning of the 17th century.

St Agnes's Chapel contains three anonymous 17th-century works depicting *St Agnes*, *St Emerentiana* and *St Constance*. In the centre of the altar is a small 17th-century Mexican crucifix made from sugar cane paste.

Finally, the *Organist's Glass Case* displays a 17th-century Christ, several 17th- and 18th-century miniatures and images of *St Anthony of Padua* and *Blessed Nicholas Factor*, 17th-century Spanish works.

By the door leading to the antechoir is a *Christ Child* seated in a chair. The nuns call this late 17th-century work *The Little Doorkeeper* owing to its location.

work by the Madrid school. Of particular interest is the *Neapolitan Nativity* displayed in a large niche decorated with mural paintings. These pieces were a gift to Sister Jesualda de Borja by her sister, the widowed countess of Alba de Liste, in 1730. Of the paintings that hang in this chapel, special mention should be made of the *Salome with the Head of John the Baptist*, a fine copy of Cesare da Sesto's originals in the Kunsthistorisches Museum in Vienna and London's National Gallery.

In the corner of the cloister is an interesting painting of the *Duke and Duchess of Styria Surrounded by their Children*. This votive work is thought to have been commissioned by Queen Margaret of Austria, Philip III's wife. Maria of Bavaria is depicted kneeling and dressed as a

▲ *St Joseph's Chapel. Upper Cloister.*

The antechoir

A large door with Plateresque woodcarvings, originally from the palace, leads to the antechoir, which contains three chapels. The *Chapel of Our Lady of El Puig* on the right-hand side contains a boxwood image of *Our Lady and the Child* which dates from the late 15th century. This sculpture was brought from Gandía by the first nuns who lived in the convent. The chapel's interior is decorated with canvases depicting scenes from *The Life of the Virgin Mary*. They were painted by Domingo Truchado in 1649.

The Marian image in the *Chapel of Our Lady of Peace* is an example of the so-called *alcuza* type (an *alcuza* is a cone-shaped vessel). The face and hands of these images are made of carved wood and the rest of the body consists of a wooden or wire structure that is specially designed to be clothed. Both the sculpture and the decoration of the chapel date from the 17th century.

The last of the three chapels is dedicated to *St Anthony* and contains an interesting 17th-century polychrome wood image based on a drawing by the Blessed Nicholas Factor, the community's confessor, who had seen a vision of the saint. The glass-enclosed altars on either side of the chapel are dedicated to the *Christ of Forgiveness* and the *Christ of the Agony*.

The display cases hold small sculptures, gold and silver articles and textiles. Particularly noteworthy are the bronze, enamel and coral altar vessels fashioned in Palermo in the first half

18th-century Neapolitan Nativity. St Michael's Chapel. Upper Cloister. ▲

of the 17th century, and the reliquaries dating from the 15th to the 17th centuries, including two 15th-century arm-reliquaries containing the relics of St Barbara and St Sebastian. Other important works are the 17th-century bronze *Christ on the Cross* by Giambologna and the small portuguese mother-of-pearl chests dating from the end of the 16th century.

Of the paintings, mention should be made of: *The Seven Archangels*, a 17th-century work attributed to Massimo Stanzione; *Our Lady of the Helpless*, the patron saint of Valencia, signed by Tomás Yepes in 1644; and several devotional pictures of Mary, such as the two representing *Our Lady of Antigua*, which are copies of the original housed in Seville Cathedral.

The panels of Talavera de la Reina tiles on the floor date from the 16th and 17th centuries.

The choir

The community of nuns gathers several times a day to pray in this room, which is located on a raised level at the west end of the church. It contains the tombs of the Empress Maria and her daughter, the Infanta Margarita. The first, fashioned in grey marble by Giovanni Battista Crescenzi, dates from the 17th century. That of the infanta, which is much simpler, is made of wood with gilt adornments such as the magnificent carving of a *Mater Dolorosa* executed by Pedro de Mena in the 17th century. The tombstones were commissioned by Philip IV and are dedicated to the memory of the Empress Maria and the Infanta Margarita.

The portrait above the entrance showing *Juana of Austria* with a dog on her lap is

▲ *View of the antechoir.*

Antechoir: top left, image of St Anthony; right, Our Lady of the Helpless, *by Tomás Yepes;* ▲
below, The Seven Archangels, *by Massimo Stanzione.*

attributed to Sánchez Coello. The other portrait is of *Maria of Portugal*, whose betrothal to Philip II was annulled in favour of Mary Tudor and led to her becoming known as "the abandoned bride".

The two altars dedicated to the *Immaculate Conception* and *Mary Mother of God* are decorated with fronts of 16th and 17th-century Talavera tiles.

A number of paintings hang above the choir stalls. The most interesting ones are: the portrait of *St Teresa of Jesus* attributed to Fray Juan de la Miseria; the *Holy Face of Christ*, a 17th-century work based on the original portrait that King Abgar of Edessa entrusted to an artist and was miraculously created by the radiation of Christ's face (an *acheiropoietos* image, not made by human hand); and the picture of *St Isidore at Prayer before Our Lady of Atocha*, a 17th-century work by the Madrid school.

The two reliefs in bronze and lapis lazuli above the choir rail depict *St Rose of Lima*; they

▲ *Pedro de Mena:* Mater Dolorosa. *Polychrome woodcarving. Choir.*

are Italian works fashioned by the circle of Melchiore Caffa at the end of the 17th century.

The splendid lectern is decorated with Renaissance woodcarvings and supports an ivory *Christ on the Cross* that belonged to St Francis Borgia.

The Upper Cloister. East and north wings

Returning to the cloister, we come to another series of chapels. The first, dedicated to the *Immaculate Conception*, contains a 17th-century woodcarving of the Virgin Mary.

The next chapel, dedicated to *Our Lady of Guadalupe*, is the richest of all those located in the cloister. Sister Ana Dorotea commissioned its decoration to the artist Sebastián Herrera Barnuevo, who completed it in 1653. The panels are painted in oil on mirrors and depict scenes from the lives of the *Strong Women of the Bible* and allegories taken from the Old Testament. The altar front, made of wood, bronze and mirrors, shows the Virgin surrounded by angels with the sun and moon in the background. The original image disappeared in the 19th century and was replaced by a 16th-century lead sculpture of the Virgin.

The *Chapel of St Francis of Paola* is dedicated to the worship of this Italian saint, who lived as a hermit and founded the Order of the Minims.

The *Chapel of Our Lady of the Angels* contains a reproduction of the image of the Virgin who appeared at Porziuncula, the chapel where St Clare was professed and where the Franciscan Order of St Clare originated. The sculpture of the Virgin is a Spanish woodcarving and dates from the 17th century. The paintings depict scenes from the life of St Francis.

Next to this chapel is an anonymous 16th-century painting showing *Cardinal Jiménez de Cisneros* during the conquest of Oran in 1509.

View of the north wing of the Upper Choir towards the main staircase. ▲

The *Ecce Homo Chapel* has an interesting late 16th-century sculpture fashioned from corn paste by the Tarasco Indians of Mexico. The walls are decorated with canvases which were signed and dated by Domingo Truchado in 1648 and depict angels and archangels.

The northeast corner of the cloister is richly adorned with murals, small display cases, sculptures and paintings, notable examples of which are the lead *Ecce Homo*, the Philippine ivory *Crucifix* and a copy of the *Holy Shroud*. The mural depicts two saints, who are identified as *St Elizabeth of Hungary* and *St Albert of Liege*.

In the north wing there is a small glass case, which, although dedicated to the Christ of St Teresa (an image originating from the church of Zimapán in Mexico), is in fact known as the *Girls' Showcase*. It owes its name to the fact that its upkeep was entrusted to the girls who lived at the convent, just as the nuns were responsible for the other chapels.

The *Chapel of the Guardian Angel* is presided over by a statue that is traditionally attributed to Luisa Roldán, "La Roldana", sculptress to Charles II. The chapel doors were a gift from the Infanta Margarita in 1620.

The display cabinet of *Our Lady of Montaigu* is dedicated to the worship of a Marian image that originated from Flanders and was disseminated by the Archduke Albert and his wife Isabella, who built a sanctuary at Scherpenheuvel (Notre Dame de Montaigu), near Brussels. The polychrome wax image, which dates from the 17th century, is designed to be dressed and its iconography does not Match that of Our Lady of Montaigu. Beneath the Virgin is a woodcarving of the *Christ Child with Instruments of the Passion*, which contains a relic of the Holy Crib and is attributed to Pedro de Mena. The bronze diptych with portraits of *St Teresa* and *St Ignatius Loyola*

commemorates the canonisation of these saints in 1622.

The following chapel is dedicated to *Our Lady of Refuge*, who is depicted in a magnificent painting attributed to Bernardino Luini. This 16th-century panel painting was presented to the convent as a gift to Sister Ana Dorotea from Queen Mariana of Austria. The smaller of the two wood and ivory *Calvaries* is 16th century, possibly French. The larger one is a 17th-century Spanish work with evident Philippine influence.

Around the doorway leading to the upper floor are several anonymous 17th-century paintings of the *Holy Family*, renderings of *St Agnes* and *St Catherine*, and a scene of the *Ship of Salvation*, all 17th-century Spanish works.

Second floor

The Staircase of the Redeemer

The door leading to the staircase dates from the 16th century and is fashioned from wood decorated with linenfold or parchemin motifs. The landing is adorned with several paintings, such as *St Joseph and the Child*, an original work by Matías de Torres dated 1696, and the 17th-century St Alexius.

On the altar is a mural depicting the *Virgin Mary Surrounded by Archangels*. This valuable work dates back to the early decoration of the convent in the second half of the 16th century and is inspired by Raphael's *Madonna of the Fish*, which hung in the Palacio de Ribera in Valladolid. Juana of Austria's facial features can be identified in this painting, in which the artist used a person as a model for a saint.

The Tapestry Room

Since 1970 this large T-shaped room has housed ten of the twenty tapestries that

Sebastián Herrera Barnuevo: Chapel of Our Lady of Guadalupe. Upper Cloister. ▶

SURGERE QUAM CERNIS SPECIOSIS CULTIBUS ARA
MENTIS HONOS ANIMI PIGNUS AMORIS OPUS
QUOS HEROINÆ SACRÆ PEPERERE TRIUMPHOS
MARIÆ ADSCRIBIT LAUDIBUS ARTE POTENS
FILIA KODUICH PIETATE INSIGNIS, ET ARMIS,
NOBILIOR CHRISTO QUAM DOROTHE DICATA
PLENA POLI HOC VNO TOT VIVEN NOMINE GESTA
NI MARIÆ ARET NON HABITURA DECUS.
ANNO. M.DC.L.III.

comprise the *Triumph of the Eucharist* series, which was given to the convent by Isabella Clara Eugenia in the first third of the 17th century. Sir Peter Paul Rubens was commissioned to do the cartoons and the tapestries were woven in Brussels at the workshops of Jan Raes, Jacques Fobert, Jean Vervoert and Jacques Geubels. The tapestries exhibited in this room depict *The Triumph of the Eucharist over Idolatry*, *The Prophet Elijah Comforted by an Angel*, *Manna in the Desert*, *The Four Evangelists*, *The Defenders of the Eucharist*, *Allegory of Franciscan Asceticism*, *Charity Enlightened by Dogma*, *Wisdom Inspired by the Holy Spirit*, and *The Triumph of the Eucharist over Ignorance and Blindness* and *The Civil and Ecclesiastic Hierarchies at Worship*. Between the last two tapestries stands a 17th-century Mexican *Christ on the Cross* fashioned from cane paste.

By the tapestries hang three portraits: *Juana of Austria*, a 17th-century work; *Isabella Clara Eugenia* dressed as a Franciscan tertiary, painted according to a model created by Rubens; and a portrait painted by Antonio Ricci in 1603 of the *Infanta Margarita*, who received the tapestries at the convent.

The large painting of the *Calvary* belongs to the 17th-century Madrid school.

Mezzanine

The Room of the Guardian Angel

The walls of this room are covered with paintings. These include: *St Bruno*, a canvas attributed to Angelo Nardi and dated to the first half of the 17th century; *St Francisco at Prayer*, a 17th-century Spanish painting; and *St Augustine Meditating on the Trinity*, a large canvas which is

▲ *View of the Tapestry Room towards the Staircase of the Redeemer and room projecting at right angles.*

attributed to Antiveduto della Grammatica and is also from the 17th century. Other notable works are *Our Lady of Sorrows*, a late 16th-century work inspired by Flemish engravings, and a painting with the faces of *SS. Peter and Paul*, a 17th-century work by the circle of Ribera.

A painting of the *Archangel Jehudiel*, attributed to Gaspar Becerra, hangs in a prominent place in the *Chapel of the Guardian Angel*. Pope Pius V granted the nuns the privilege of holding a solemn mass at this chapel every year on 23 August.

The Cell of the Infanta Margarita

This small room was inhabited by Margarita of Austria, the youngest daughter of the Empress Maria, who was a nun of this convent and is buried in the choir. The room contains some of her personal belongings.

Tapestry Room. Top, view from the Staircase of the Redeemer; bottom, Antonio Ricci: The Infanta Margarita. ▲

The glass cases contain a *Nativity* in coral, silver, copper and enamel made in the Neapolitan town of Trapani. It appears to be a gift to the convent from Philip II. The *Sleeping Christ Child* seated on a "friar's chair" and dressed in the style of the young infantes is a late 16th-century Spanish work.

The "Candilón"

When one of the nuns died, the whole community held a wake beside her body in this room, which was illuminated by a large brazier or *candil* from which its name was derived. Part of the convent's fine collection of portraits is currently exhibited here.

Thirteen paintings decorate this room. Near the entrance are portraits of *The Infantes Don Diego and Don Felipe* signed by Alonso Sánchez Coello in 1579 and *The Infantas Isabella Clara Eugenia and Catalina Micaela*, also painted by Sánchez Coello between 1568 and 1569. These two canvases show four of Philip II's children, the princes born to his last wife, Anne of Austria, and the two princesses born of his marriage to Elizabeth of

▲ *Alonso Sánchez Coello:* Isabella Clara Eugenia and Catalina Micaela, *with the main facade of the former Alcázar palace in the background.* Candilón.

Top, view of the "Candilón". Bottom, Sicilian-made coral Nativity. Cell of the Infanta Margarita. ▲

Valois. Nearby is a portrait of *Sebastian of Portugal* by Cristóbal de Morales, signed and dated in 1565. It shows the only son of Juana of Austria and Prince John of Portugal at the age of eleven.

On the following wall hangs the portrait of the *Infante Don Ferdinand*, also by Sánchez Coello and dated 1577. Ferdinand was the first son of Philip II and Anne of Austria and was six years old when he sat for this portrait.

Above the altar is a 17th-century woodcarving of *St Clare*, which is attributed to Gregorio Fernández.

Further along are the portraits of *John of Austria*, by Sánchez Coello, *Juana of Austria*, by the same artist, and the *Prince Don Carlos*, by Cristóbal de Morales. They all date from the second half of the 16th century.

Another group of portraits shows the brother and sisters of the Emperor Charles V: *Ferdinand I* of Germany; *Eleonor of Austria*, queen of France and Portugal; and *Catherine of Portugal*. Beside them is the portrait of *Mary of Portugal*, the daughter of Emanel of Portugal and Eleonor of Austria. They are all attributed to Sir Anthony More.

Finally, there is a portrait of *Marie Louise de Villars*, the French ambassador's daughter. The portrait, which was altered at some point to depict Marie as St Lucy, is signed by Luis Ferdinand and dated 1676. The portrait believed to show an infante as the *Christ Child* is an example of the late 16th-century trend of portraying people as saints.

The sculpture of the *Christ Child with Instruments of the Passion* asleep below a baldachin belongs to the 17th-century Castilian school.

The 17th-century chest-bureaus are Mexican and are decorated with scenes fashioned in lacquer.

▲ *"Candilón". Top, Cristóbal de Morales:* Sebastian of Portugal; *bottom, Alonso Sánchez Coello:* John of Austria.

The Chapter House

A door with Plateresque woodcarvings leads into this room where the chapter formerly met to discuss community matters of particular importance.

The pictorial decoration consists of trompe l'oeil mural paintings representing mock architectural structures. They are 17th-century works by the school of Madrid. Among them are 14 canvases nailed to the wall imitating frescoes. They illustrate scenes from *The Life of St Francis* in chronological order, from birth to death, and are anonymous 17th-century works.

Above the door is a mural painting of *The Crucified Nun*; this painting, of considerable iconographic significance, is an interesting depiction of certain aspects of religious life.

Some of the convent's finest sculptures are now displayed in this room. The sculpture group on the altar is entitled *St Francis Handing the Rule to St Clare* and is a 17th-century Spanish work. The display cabinets contain a *Mater Dolorosa* and an *Ecce Homo*, both magnificent examples of Andalusian imagery signed and dated by Pedro de Mena in 1673. The larger image represents a *Penitent Mary Magdalene* and is attributed to Gregorio Fernández.

Other works are the bust of a *Mater Dolorosa* by the Granada sculptor José Risueño and a *St Isabella of Portugal* by Manuel Pereira.

Chapter House. Above the altar, San Francisco Handing the Rule to St Clare. ▲

The Hall of the Kings

This hall displays a number of original decorative features of the former palace, such as a stucco frieze with plant motifs surrounding the coat of arms of Alonso Gutiérrez and a tiled dado indicating the existence of original openings that were subsequently modified.

The collection of royal portraits is exhibited on all four walls. They are arranged in the following manner:

Around the entrance are: *Sister Mariana de la Cruz y Austria*, daughter of the Cardinal Infante Don Ferdinand, an anonymous 18th-century painting; and a *Laudatory Inscription to Charles V, Philip II and Juana of Austria*. Beside them is the portrait of *Ana Dorotea of Austria*,

▲ *Hall of the Kings. Top left, Sir Peter Paul Rubens:* Sister Ana Dorotea; *right, George van der Straeten:* Elizabeth of Austria; *bottom, Pantoja de la Cruz:* The Empress Maria.

which belongs to the same series as that of *Mariana de la Cruz*. Lower down the wall is the portrait of *Archduke Ernest*, son of the Empress Maria, painted by Franz Pourbus the Younger about 1592. It is followed by the *Empress Maria*, by then a widow, next to a table on which her crown stands. It was painted by Juan Pantoja de la Cruz towards the end of the 16th century. Nearby is a painting of her daughter *Elizabeth of Austria*, the wife of Charles IX of France. This painting is signed by Georges van der Straeten and dated 1573. On the same wall hangs the portrait of Philip III's wife *Margaret of Austria*, an anonymous 17th-century Spanish work. Beside it is a portrait of her husband *Philip III* painted in the 17th century by the school of Bartolomé González. Beneath them is their daughter *Ana Mauricia of Austria* as a child,

signed by Pantoja de la Cruz and dated 1603. The remaining portraits include the *Infant of Prague*, which was painted in 1696 and given to the convent by Sister Mariana de la Cruz. Near the door is the portrait of *Sister Ana Dorotea* at the age of 17, painted by Rubens in 1628.

Finally, the portrait of *Anne of Austria*, wife of Emperor Matthias, is attributed to Hans van Aechen and was painted in the second half of the 16th century. Above the niche is *Anne of Austria-Styria*, dated 1582, which is part of a set comprising two other portraits of daughters of Archduke Charles of Styria. Originally secular portraits, they were later altered to depict saints, in this case St Agnes. The last portrait, depicting *Charles II*, is a 17th-century work of the Madrid school by the followers of Claudio Coello and Carreño de Miranda. In the niche

View of the Hall of the Kings. ▲

stands *St Michael the Archangel*, a sculpture by Luisa Roldán, a gift to the convent from Juan José of Austria.

On the wall leading to the kitchen garden hangs a portrait of *Sister Margarita de la Cruz*. This painting belongs to a series of nuns' portraits displayed in this room, as does that of Sister *Catalina de Este*. Other portraits show daughters of Archduke Charles: *Maria Christina* depicted as St Lucy and *Anne of Austria* as St Dorothy. In the centre is a painted fabric depicting *Our Lady of Loreto*.

On the following wall is a portrait of the *Archduchess Catherine*, also of the Austria-Styria family, depicted as St Catherine. It is dated 1582. The portrait of *Juana of Austria* on the upper part of the wall is a copy of an original by Sánchez Coello and displays a long biographical inscription. Below it is a painting of the *Cardinal Infante at the Battle of Nordlingen* produced by Rubens's studio. On either side hang portraits of *Juan José of Austria* and *Mariana de la Cruz*, depicted as St Hermenegild and St Ursula. They are attributed to Eugenio de las Cuevas and dated to the second half of the 17th century. Another pair of portraits painted by Franz Pourbus the Younger in 1599 show the *Archduke Albert* and *Isabella Clara Eugenia*. Lastly, there is a 17th-century *Christ Child* from the Madrid school and a portrait of *Isabella Clara Eugenia* dressed as a Franciscan tertiary, a copy of Rubens's original.

At the far end of the room stands an altarpiece comprising three vertical and two

▲ *View of the oratory.*

horizontal sections. It is decorated with paintings depicting *St Joaquin, St Anne, The Virgin and Child* and *St John the Baptist as a Child*, in addition to the scenes of *The Prayer in the Garden* and *The Resurrection of Christ*. In the centre is a sculpture of *St Clare* executed by Pedro de Mena in 1675. Near the top of the wall hang two paintings of *Groups of Nuns at Prayer*, in which some of the most renowned nuns can be identified, and between them is the *Coat of Arms of the Empress Maria*. Finally, four 16th-century Spanish panels show *Christ at the Column, The Descent from the Cross, The Prayer in the Garden* and *Christ Carrying the Cross*.

The oratory

The oratory is reached via a narrow corridor hung with portraits of *Wladyslaw* and *Anna Maria*, prince and princess of Poland and Sweden. The paintings were executed in 1596 and are attributed to Martin Kober.

The *Virgin and Child* dates from the 17th century and hails from Ribera's circle. The *Circumcision* is an 18th-century Spanish work.

Inside the oratory hangs a large *Baptism of Christ*, a late 16th-century work displaying Flemish and Italian influence. Special mention should be made of three paintings, all of them oil on copper, from the school of Rubens. They portray *SS. Joaquin and Anne with the Virgin, The Return to Nazareth* and *The Supper at Emmaus*. In the centre is a Spanish painting of *Our Lady of Sleep*.

The portrait above the entrance shows the *Blessed Nicholas Factor*, confessor of the convent; it was painted by Juan Zariñena and is dated 1577. Other works in this room are: *The Presentation of the Virgin*, a Flemish panel painting; *St Francis Comforted by Three Angels*; the *Pietà*, which displays the influence of

El Greco; and a 17th-century Spanish *Christ Child with Instruments of the Passion*.

Also on display is *St Agnes*, an oil painting on canvas signed by Antonio Salazar in 1614. Beside it are *The Last Supper* and *St Luis Beltrán before the Virgin*. Beltrán was a Dominican saint from Valencia to whom the Blessed Nicolás Factor professed deep devotion.

A long corridor decorated with paintings of *Sibyls* leads to the last rooms in the museum. The dado of Talavera tiling displaying animal scenes deserves particular attention.

The Flemish Painting Room

This room, originally part of the Royal Apartments, houses the convent's collection of Flemish painting.

On the left wall hangs the *Ship of the Church and the Port of Salvation*; this work is of great iconographic interest and clearly reminiscent of Bosch. Although 16th-century in style, it

MEZZANINE

Prince Wladislao, attributed to Martin Kober, 1596. Oratory corridor. ▲

▲ *Flemish Painting Room: top,* The Ship of the Church and the Port of Salvation. *Follower of Bosch. 16th and 17th century; bottom,* Our Lady with a Parrot, *attributed to Adriaen Isenbrant.*

appears to have been painted in the first decades of the 17th century.

On the next wall is a *Holy Family with Musical Angels*, a 16th-century work by the Bruges school. It is followed by a large painting by Rubens's school depicting *Our Lady Handing the Child to St Francis*. Below it is the *Pilgrimage of Archduke Albert and Isabella to Laeken*, an interesting record of one of the governors' many visits to the sanctuary of Laeken outside Brussels. The work is signed by Jan van der Beken and dated 1601. Above the door is *St Luke Drawing a Portrait of the Virgin Mary*, a fine copy of Roger van der Weyden's original housed in the Museum of Fine Arts in Boston.

The next wall displays a *Calvary* and an *Adoration of the Shepherds*, both anonymous 16th-century works. Above them is *Our Lady of the Grapes*, a 16th-century work by a follower of Joos van Cleve. In the centre is *Our Lady with a Parrot*; this painting, which is attributed to Adriaen Isenbrandt, belonged to the private collection of Juana of Austria, who wished it to be placed above her tomb. To the right is the *Adoration of the Magi*, a fine triptych by Pieter Coecke van Aelst dating from the first half of the 16th century. Above it is *Christ with the Virgin and St John*, a free interpretation attributed to Jan Gossaert of the top panel of the Van Eyck brothers' polyptych of the *Adoration of the Lamb* in the church of St Bavon in Ghent. To the right is a painting of *St Cecilia*, the patron saint of music, by Michel Coxcie.

Above the door hangs an oil on panel of an *Ecce Homo* painted by Juan de Justo in 1496. To the right is a Flemish panel painting of *The Last Supper* and a home altarpiece with *Passion* scenes attributed to Marcellus Coffermans.

The *St Jerome* on the adjacent wall is painted according to the iconography made popular by Marinus van Reymerswaele. It is followed by a detailed rendering of

Room of Spanish and Italian Painting: top, The Tribute Money, *by Titian; bottom,* Face of a Nun, *Madrid school.* ▲

The Martyrdom of St Ursula and the Eleven Thousand Virgins painted by Giulio Licinio around 1558. This painting may have arrived at the convent with the relics of the eleven thousand virgins sent from Cologne by the Emperor Ferdinand I. Near the top is an Adoration of the Magi attributed to Pieter Brueghel the Elder.

The Room of Spanish and Italian Painting

Above the door are: a Christ Carrying the Cross by Sebastiano del Piombo dated c. 1520; a 17th-century St Jerome Penitent attributed to Francisco de Solís; an Adoration of the Magi signed by Eugenio Horozco dating from the second half of the 17th century; a St Francis Penitent displaying the influence of the circle of Morales "the Divine"; and a 17th-century Mater Dolorosa attributed to Carlo Dolci. Another Christ Carrying the Cross is also attributed to Sebastiano del Piombo. These paintings are followed by The Birth of the Virgin and The Archangels Presenting the Child, a pair of canvases by Luca Giordano. The small sketch of the Empress Maria above the fireplace is reminiscent of the style of Francisco de Goya. Above it is St Francis in Glory, a sketch by Antonio González Velázquez for the decoration of the church's ceiling.

On the adjacent wall is a 17th-century portrait of St Margaret attributed to Cecco da Caravaggio. In the centre is The Tribute Money, an oil painting on panel signed by Titian. To the right hangs The Annunciation, a

  ▲ Luca Giordano: The Archangels with the Child. Room of Spanish and Italian Painting.

17th-century work by the Neapolitan artist Fabrizio Santafede.

The first painting on the following wall is a *St Francis* attributed to Francisco Zurburán. *St Peter* is dated 1591 and signed by Andrea Lilio of Ancona. *St Sebastian* was painted by Pedro Orrente about 1606, and *St Anthony* is attributed to El Greco's son Jorge Manuel. The last of the paintings on this wall is the *Face of a Nun*, a splendid portrait that is similar in style to the works produced by the 17th-century Madrid school.

On the last wall hangs *The Immaculate Conception*, signed by Francisco Fernández in 1664. To the left is *The Virgin and Child*, possibly painted by Morales the Divine, and to the right another *Immaculate Conception*, this one a copy of a work by Ribera and attributed to Francisco Solís.

The church

THE BLESSED Sacrament was placed in the newly built church on 8 December 1564. The works were supervised by the architect Juan Bautista de Toledo, whose influence can be clearly seen in the church's main facade. A number of artists, including Gaspar Becerra, Antonio Sillero, Juan Gómez de Mora and Diego Villanueva, worked on the interior.

Two chapels dedicated to St Sebastian and St John the Baptist stand on either side of the nave in the manner of transepts. They contain paintings of the saints, executed on marble by Gaspar Becerra. These particular saints were chosen in remembrance of Sebastian and John of Portugal, son and husband of Juana of Austria.

View of the church. ▲

The railings enclosing the chapels were crafted by Gaspar Rodríguez in 1574. The bronze rail in front of the presbytery, which was brought from Flanders in 1613, was made some years later.

The church's original altarpiece with sculptures and paintings was made by Gaspar Becerra about 1565. Diego Villanueva refurbished the interior in the 17th century. Around the same time the doors to the chaplains' cloister were added and the González Velázquez brothers executed the frescoes for the ceiling vault. Unfortunately, on 15 October 1862 a fire destroyed most of the church and almost completely ruined the decoration of the presbytery, where Pantoja de la Cruz's portraits of the *Empress Maria* and *Juana of Austria* and Gaspar Becerra's altarpiece were located.

The church was rebuilt on a low budget – a fact which conditioned the new decoration. A new altarpiece from the former Jesuit novitiate in Madrid was placed in the presbytery. This work, fashioned from marble by Camilo Rusconi, depicts *The Ecstasy of St Francis Regis.* In order to adapt the altarpiece to its new site, six stucco reliefs of Franciscan saints had to be added on either side as well as a stucco high relief of *The Assumption* at the top.

In front of the altarpiece is an image of *Our Lady of the Miracle* by Paolo de San Leocadio. It was a gift from a hermit to Doña Leonor de Borja, who gave it to her sister Juana, a nun at the Convent of Santa Clara in Gandía. The first community of nuns brought it with them to Madrid from Valencia.

The current portraits of *Juana* and *Maria of Austria* were painted by Pedro Pardo and are dated 1863. The vault was redecorated according to surviving sketches by the González Velázquez brothers. The church's present appearance is a result of the restoration work carried out in 1989 and 1990.

After Juana died at the Monastery of San Lorenzo de El Escorial, her last wishes – to rest in the convent she had founded – were fulfilled. A section of her apartments to the right of the main altar was converted into a burial chapel. Different artists took part in these works, though the architect Juan de Herrera and the marble mason Jacome a Trezzo were mainly responsible for the chapel, which houses Pompeo Leoni's magnificent white marble *sculpture of the princess kneeling in prayer*.

The church's sober facade is made of brick and granite. The upper section bears the coat of arms, carved out of stone, of Juana of Austria.

The tour of the Convent of Las Descalzas Reales provides visitors with an insight into significant aspects of Spanish and European history. It also gives them the opportunity to enjoy an exceptional museum through which

▲ *J. de Herrera, J. da Trezzo and P. Leoni.* Tomb of Juana of Austria. *Church.*

View of the Relics Chapel. ▶

the community of Poor Clares convey the way of life they have maintained for centuries in accordance with their founder's wishes.

Rooms in the enclosed area

IN ADDITION to the rooms that are included in the tour, there are a number which are usually closed to the public. However, they deserve a mention on account of their great historical and artistic importance.

The Relics Chapel

The Hall of the Kings leads to this small room which has been used to display relics since early times. It was established by the convent's founder, Juana of Austria, and occupies part of one of the rooms of the former palace where Empress Isabella of Portugal lived and Juana was born.

Arranged on shelves inside the display cabinets are a number of relics in luxurious reliquaries. These were either sent to the convent from Rome by Juana, brought from Germany by the Empress Maria or donated by members of the royal family. Some of these reliquaries are exceptional works of art, such as the 17th-century *ostensory* containing a relic of the lignum crucis or wood from Christ's cross, which was adorned with gold on the orders of the Emperor Maximilian II.

Also worthy of mention are the **small chests** which were once jewel boxes, travelling cases or belonged to writing desks and were converted

▲ Recumbent Virgin *surrounded by* The Twelve Apostles *and* St Paul. *Chapel of the Dormition.*

into reliquaries after arriving at the convent. They include a silver *chest* fashioned by the silversmith Wenzel Jamnitzer in 1570. This item was part of the trousseau of Anne of Austria, Philip II's wife, who gave it to her aunt, Juana of Austria, in 1571. Originally a jewellery case, it has since housed the relics of St Victor.

An equally interesting piece is the wood and silver *chest*, a 17th-century Florentine jewellery case which contains a relic of St Francis Borgia. The wooden *chest* decorated with relief work, silver sculptures and cameos was made in Rome in the 17th century and now houses the skull of St Cecilia.

Also noteworthy are the *exotic chests* from Mexico, Japan and India. The wooden box with marquetry hunting scenes was made by Bartholomeus Weisshaupt in 1577.

The Relics Chapel also contains a number of 17th-century **bust-reliquaries** and a fine collection of **small paintings and reliefs**. Mention should also be made of the **coral reliefs** from Sicily and the Mexican shell pictures of the Virgin Mary and St Joseph. The frieze of Talavera tiles imitates the Andalusian style.

The Chapel of the Dormition

The Tapestry Room, once the nuns' dormitory, leads to three small rooms which contain interesting works of art. The first was originally known as the *Room of the Assumption* and is dedicated to the Transition of the Virgin.

This markedly Mediterranean image was brought to the convent by the first community of nuns from the Convent of Santa Clara in Gandía. In the dimly lit chapel the *recumbent figure of the Virgin* is watched over by the apostles. The figure is designed to be dressed and only the face, hands and feet are carved; the rest of the body consists of a wooden structure over which the Virgin's numerous garments are placed. It dates from the early 17th century, though the garments now worn were made in the 18th century.

Surrounding the image of the Virgin are sculptures of the *Twelve Apostles* and *St Paul*. These polychrome woodcarvings date from the early 18th century and are similar in style to others of the Andalusian school. The figure of *St James the Apostle* is painted, not carved; tradition has it that he had already been martyred by the time Mary died and his presence was therefore spiritual rather than physical.

Above the display case containing the Virgin is a mural painting of *Our Lady of Montserrat*, to whom the Infanta Margarita professed great devotion. Several paintings hang on the upper section of the walls, including an anonymous 17th-century portrait of *Sister María Jesús de Agreda* and a portrait of *St Gertrudis the Great*, a 17th-century work by an anonymous Spanish artist. The room also contains an anonymous 17th-century Spanish painting of *St Sebastian Martyred*.

The religious paintings that hang in this room include: an *Annunciation* signed by Vincenzo Carducci and dated 1624; a copy of *Our Lady of Antigua*, a 17th-century work from Seville; an 18th-century *Adoration of the Shepherds* attributed to Luis Meléndez; an anonymous 16th-century Flemish *Jesus Among the Doctors*; and *Rest on the Flight into Egypt*, an anonymous late 17th-century Spanish work.

The chapel ceiling is covered by a large canvas in the manner of a fresco depicting *The Assumption of the Virgin*. This painting, executed by Luca Giordano, dates from the last quarter of the 17th century.

A niche located between this and the next room contains an interesting 17th-century sculptural group of *St Anne, St Joaquim and Our Lady as a Girl*.

The Holy House of Nazareth

One of the most original rooms in the convent, the Holy House of Nazareth contains half-hidden evidence of the former palace's architectural structure. Before the building was converted into a convent, this area had a wide upper gallery in the style of 16th-century Castilian courtyards with stone columns and capitals and wooden bases. When the gallery was walled up the columns became embedded in the wall. A replica of the *Holy House of Nazareth* – the scene of the Annunciation, which was miraculously borne by angels to the Italian town of Loreto – was built in the resulting room. Both the outer and inner walls of this small, single-roomed house are hung with paintings. The gable roof is made of polychrome wood.

Although the House was built in the late 16th or early 17th century, the pictures were not painted and hung until the middle of the 17th century. The paintings inside the House are Renaissance in style and depict scenes from the *Childhood of Christ* framed by decorative borders. Beneath the masonry altar on the east side is an *Adoration of the Shepherds*; the trompe l'oeil paintings on either side depict the objects used in the celebration of Holy Mass. Above the altar, an anonymous 16th-century *Annunciation* recalls the event that took place in this House. The mural paintings covering the outer walls form a large frieze depicting saints associated with the Franciscan Order –

Antechapel of the Miracle showing scenes from The Childhood of Christ. *View from the arch of the Chapel of the Miracle.* ▶

St Anthony and *St Clare* – and with the convent's founder, Juana of Austria, such as *St Sebastian* and *SS John* by Francisco Rizi.

The decorative paintwork – the dado and skirting board – was carried out by Dionisio Mantuano, a Bolognese painter and architect who worked in Spain from 1656 and was appointed painter to King Philip IV in 1665. His signature can be seen on the lower part of the west wall.

When it arrived at the convent, the painting of *Our Lady of the Miracle* was placed inside the House, where it remained until 1678, the year the splendid chapel to which it gives its name was completed. Thereafter the House, previously a free-standing construction, became attached to the south wall of the new chapel dedicated to Our Lady of the Miracle.

The walls of the room in which the Holy House is located are hung with paintings depicting religious themes. Three of them represent different Marian images: *Our Lady of the Rosary*, *Our Lady of the Sacrarium of Toledo* and *Our Lady of the Foundling Home*. Other paintings depict: *The Calling of SS Peter and Andrew*, a 17th-century copy of an original by Barocci; an anonymous 16th-century Italian *Pietà*; and an anonymous 17th-century Spanish *Calvary*.

The Chapel of the Miracle

This small chapel is one of the finest examples of 17th-century mural paintings that exist in Madrid. Royal patronage played a major role in its origins, as it was Don Juan José of Austria, a natural son of Philip IV, who

▲ *Paintings of saints and door leading to the Antechapel of the Miracle. Holy House of Nazareth.*

◀ The Coronation of the Virgin by the Trinity, *on the dome, and* The Royal Window of Charles II and Juan José of Austria, *on the left-hand lunette. Chapel of the Miracle.*

Carved gilt wood altarpiece. Chapel of the Miracle. ▲

promoted and financed its construction in 1678. It is therefore one of the few surviving monuments dating from the short period in which Charles II's stepbrother politically dominated Spain.

Don Juan decided to finance the building of this chapel as a gift to his natural daughter Margarita, whose mother was Rosa Ribera, the daughter of the great painter José Ribera. Margarita took her vows in the Convent of Las Descalzas Reales in 1666 at the age of sixteen, becoming known as Sister Margarita de la Cruz.

The Madrid court was especially devoted to Our Lady of the Miracle in the 17th century. The painting was brought to the convent in the 16th century by the first nuns, who came from the Convent of Santa Clara in Gandía. The image had been bequeathed by a hermit to Leonor de Borja, daughter of the duke and duchess of Gandía. Doña Leonor venerated the image in her palace chapel, where it inspired deep devotion and became known throughout the kingdom of Valencia for the miracles it worked. Leonor bequeathed the painting to her sister, Juana de la Cruz, then a nun at the Convent of Santa Clara in Gandía and subsequently the first abbess of Las Descalzas Reales in Madrid. It thus found its way into the convent and was hung in the Holy House of Nazareth, remaining there until 1678, when it was transferred to its new chapel. The chapel is divided into two rooms, an ante-chapel and the chapel proper. It is reached through a wooden door imitating a gilded bronze screen, which displays the Virgin Mary's monogram and a Maltese Cross representing the patronage of Juan José of Austria, the order's Grand Prior in Spain.

Both rooms are entirely covered in mural paintings in fresco, oil and tempera. They depict scenes framed by trompe l'oeil buildings and sculptures. In the ante-chapel, which stands on a rectangular plan and has a flat ceiling vault, the walls are decorated with scenes in oil of the childhood of Christ: *The Flight into Egypt*, *The Presentation in the Temple*, *The Nativity* and *The Adoration of the Magi*.

A large archway connecting the two rooms leads to the chapel, which has a square ground plan and a domed ceiling supported by pendentives. Murals cover the walls. The mock architecture emphasises the symmetry of the area and frames scenes such as *The Presentation of the Virgin in the Temple*, *The Annunciation* and the chapel of the *SS John*, and also supports mock sculptures of *The Cardinal Virtues*. A particularly interesting feature of this chapel is the so-called *Royal Window* showing Charles II in the foreground and behind him Juan José of Austria, both in prayer.

The pendentives display *St Clare*, *St Elizabeth of Hungary*, *St Anthony* and *St Francis*. The central theme on the dome is *The Coronation of the Virgin by the Trinity*. Other scenes include *St Michael*, angels, *King David Playing the Harp*, *Jacob's Ladder* and *The Ark of the Covenant*. Around the base of the dome runs a mock rail over which figures look down.

The chapel was decorated by Francisco Rizi and Dionisio Mantuano. Rizi was responsible for the scenes, and Mantuano executed the mock architecture, trompe l'oeil and other decorative elements.

On the east wall is a large carved wood and gilded altarpiece with a painting of *Our Lady of the Miracle* in the centre. This picture is a copy of Paolo de San Leocadio's original, which is now in the convent's public church. Four sculptures flank the central niche: on one side the archangels *St Michael* and *St Gabriel*, and on the other *St Margaret* and *St Dorothy*.

The upper section of the altarpiece is adorned with a 17th-century painting of *The Visitation of Mary to St Elizabeth*.

Gold and silverwork, paintings and prints

Mention should be made of a number of works of art which, although kept in the enclosed area, are very significant. Such is the case of the **gold and silver items**, such as the *monstrance* in which the Blessed Sacrament is displayed on Good Friday, when it is placed in the shrine that houses the image of the *Recumbent Christ*. Tradition has it that it was a gift from King Charles II in the late 17th century. It is made of gilded silver and adorned with pearls, diamonds and enamel. Also of note is the gilded silver *chalice* decorated with emeralds, which belonged to Sister Ana Dorotea.

Noteworthy among the paintings is *The Last Supper*, which hangs in the Refectory and is similar in style to the works of Juan de Juanes.

Last but not least is the convent's large and valuable collection of prints. Along with the Zamora and Albert collections housed in the Biblioteca Nacional, it is one of the best holdings of monastic devotional prints. It includes works dating from the 16th to the 20th centuries and techniques range from engraving to photomechanical reproductions. Notable works are a 16th-century *Passion* engraved by Albrecht Dürer, the allegorical prints (some of the copperplates for which still survive) by the Wierix brothers, also dating from the 16th century, and the *Litanies of Loreto* executed by the Klauber family of engravers in the 18th century.

Albrecht Dürer: The Taking of Christ *or* The Kiss of Judas, *1508 (left);* Christ, Man of Suffering, *1509 (right).* ▲
Passion series. Print collection. Enclosure.

The Convent of
La Encarnación

THE CONVENT of La Encarnación in Madrid was founded in 1611 by Philip III and Margaret of Austria. Seeing the result of the work carried out by Princess Juana of Portugal at Las Descalzas Reales, the queen decided to have a similar convent built near the Alcázar palace. While Valladolid was the seat of the Court (1600-1606), Queen Margaret founded a number of important religious institutions, including a Jesuit School in Salamanca. It was precisely in Valladolid that she heard that an Augustinian nun, Mariana de San José, was carrying out a reform of the nuns of the Order of St Augustine together with Agustín Antolínez, then provincial of Castile and subsequently archbishop of Santiago. Mariana de San José seemed to the queen to be a suitable prioress for the new convent in Madrid and Margaret therefore decided to summon her to Madrid and place her in charge of the community of nuns who were to live in the future Convent of La Encarnación. Mariana de San José accepted Margaret's offer and, after being granted authorisation from the bishop of Palencia – at the time she was living at a convent in Palencia – and from the provincial of the Order of St Augustine, she took up residence in Madrid together with three nuns from Valladolid, who were progressively joined by others.

The site chosen for the convent was located opposite the Colegio de Doña María de Aragón (now the Senate) and the royal architect Juan Gómez de Mora was commissioned to design the building. The convent was connected with the Alcázar palace by a passageway running between one of the wings of the main facade and the Casa del Tesoro (Palace Treasury) next to the Alcázar. The first stone was laid in 1611 and the building was completed in 1616. While the convent was being built, the nuns lived first at the Convent of Santa Isabel (1612, in Calle Santa Isabel) and subsequently at the Casa del Tesoro (1613-1616).

Queen Margaret died at El Escorial in 1611 and it was Philip III who saw to the completion of the building. The convent was governed by the charters of foundation issued by Philip III in 1618, the charter issued by Philip IV in 1625 endorsing those of his father; and by the Augustinian Rule of 1616. Both ordinances were ratified by papal bulls issued by Paul V in 1618 and by Gregory XV in 1625. The Convent of La Encarnación was conceived as a prime exponent of the Catholic Church as it embodied the reforms carried out by the Council of Trent.

The fire that destroyed the Hapsburg Alcázar palace in 1734 severed the link between the royal palace and the convent, since the new palace, which was built at right angles to the earlier building, was not connected with the Casa del Tesoro.

During the Bonapartist rule the Plaza de Oriente was remodelled and the passageway and the Casa del Tesoro were demolished. Later, in 1810, La Encarnación was included on the list convents doomed to disappear as it lacked the minimum number of nuns stipulated in the decree governing the dissolution of convents.

◀ *View of the main section of the facade showing the forecourt of the church of La Encarnación.*

Between 1842 and 1847 the community was forced to vacate the building following the Disentailment Act of 1836. Once the nuns were evicted, the complex began to be demolished and only the church, the cloister and a few of the adjacent buildings were left standing. Shortly afterwards it was decided to halt the demolition works and rebuild the convent according to the designs of the palace's chief architect, Narciso Pascual y Colomer. In 1844 part of the kitchen garden was divided up into plots in order to sell and develop the land for housing. As a result, it became necessary to redistribute the convent's interior in accordance with its current dimensions. The facades were built in 17th-century Madrid style rather than being adapted to neoclassical tastes.

In 1868 the convent took in other communities of nuns who had been evicted from their convents as a result of the Revolution of '68. The community was again forced to vacate the building between 1936 and 1939 on account of the Civil War.

The architectural structure

THE CONVENT of La Encarnación is built in a classical style that is modelled on the designs introduced by Herrera's followers at El Escorial. The convent complex forms a large rectangle with the church at the centre; leading up to the entrance is a forecourt which separates the religious and urban areas and is enclosed on either side by walls and by railings opposite the facade. The walls are flint masonry and brick and the facade is granite. The church facade is the so-called "box" type and displays a severe geometrical design with Baroque features. It has been attributed to Juan Gómez de Mora,

View of the exterior of the Convent of La Encarnación. ▲

though some researchers believe that it was designed by Fray Aberto de la Madre de Dios.

The forerunner to the facade of La Encarnación can be seen in the Monastery of San José in Ávila, which was designed by Francisco de Mora. The Madrid facade is a rectangle formed by two plain pilasters with architraves surmounted by a straight pediment. Horizontally, it is divided into three segments: the first has a portico with three arches supported by pilasters, the central arch being the tallest and broadest; the second corresponds to the upper choir and has a recess with a relief flanked by two windows; and the third contains the coats of arms of its royal founders. The relief, carved in marble by Antonio de Riera around 1617,

depicts *The Annunciation*, to which the building is dedicated.

Ground floor

The vestibule

The entrance or vestibule where the ticket office is located has three doors: the one on the right leads to the forecourt; the left-hand door to the nuns' parlours; and the door opposite is the entrance to the Museum. The room is decorated with oil paintings on canvas depicting various Bourbon monarchs who were once patrons of the convent. The portrait of *Isabella Farnese*, Philip V's second wife, is a copy of an original by Van Loo; *Philip V* is attributed to Antonio

▲ *Nuns' Lobby.*

Palomino; *Maria Luisa of Savoy*, Philip V's first wife, is a copy of an 18th-century Italian work; *Mariana Josefa* of Austria, the dowager queen of John V of Portugal and daughter of the Emperor Leopold of Austria, was painted by Andrés de la Calleja in 1754; *Louis I* is a copy of a Spanish original painted in the 18th century; *Ferdinand VI* and *Barbara of Bragança* are copies of works by Jean Ranc; *Charles III* and *Maria Amalia of Saxony* are copies of 18th-century Neapolitan works; *Charles IV* and *Maria Luisa of Parma* are attributed to Antonio Carnicero; *Ferdinand VII* is a copy of an original by Vicente López; and the *St Joseph and the Child* is a 17th-century Spanish painting.

Between this room and the nuns' lobby is *Our Lady of the Victories*, a 19th-century woodcarving given to the convent by the Congregation of Trinitarians in Calle Marqués de Urquijo, Madrid.

The Nuns' Lobby

This room is so called because it originally contained the doors leading to the enclosed area. The original revolving window can still be seen on the right. There are four doors: the first on the left leads to one of the convent's inner courtyards; the second on the left to the Painting Room; the door opposite the entrance leads to the lower cloisters; and the door on the right to the Clock Staircase.

The most important work in the room is the canvas painted by Luca Giordano in 1657

Anonymous Flemish artist: The Exchange of Princesses on the River Bidasoa. *Nuns' Lobby.* ▲

depicting *St Augustine* and *St Monica* (known as *The Ecstasy of Ostia*, it illustrates a passage recounted in St Augustine's *Confessions*).

Another outstanding painting is *The Exchange of Princesses on the River Bidasoa*. It depicts a marriage arrangement which took place on the Isle of Pheasants on the river Bidasoa in 1615 whereby Anne of Austria, Philip III's daughter, departed for France to become the wife of Louis XIII, and Elizabeth of Bourbon, the daughter of Henry IV of France and Marie de Medici, journeyed to Spain to marry Philip IV. The exchange, which took place during the Twelve-Year Truce, led to peace between France and Spain. Several copies of the ceremony exist; most were commissioned by Marie de Medici between 1623 and 1627. This one is anonymous. It depicts the Spanish retinue on the left and the French one on the right; in the centre, two ferries convey the princesses to their future husbands. A cartouche in the lower left-hand corner lists the various elements shown in the painting. Patrimonio Nacional possesses another two similar canvases: one, an anonymous Flemish painting housed in El Escorial, forms a pair with the one in La Encarnación and shows *The Arrival of the Spanish Retinue at San Sebastián*; the other, which hangs in the Reales Alcázares in Seville, is by Van Mullen and is entitled *View of La Concha Bay*.

By the Lower Cloister hang *The Flagellation of Christ*, which is attributed to Juan de Roelas, a painter belonging to Velázquez's circle, and two works by 17th-century Florentine painters: *Christ, Man of Suffering*, by Ottavio Vannini, and *Christ Among the Blessed* by Matteo Rosselli.

Near the staircase leading to the courtyard is *Christ Among the Doctors*, a 17th-century work by the Spanish school.

On the table stands a display cabinet containing an 18th-century Spanish *St Rita*, an image designed to be dressed.

The tiled dado around the room hails from the Talavera de la Reina pottery workshops and bears the same designs as the so-called "illustrious fleuron" made by the potter Juan Fernández for the Monastery of El Escorial in 1570.

The Painting Room

This room contains a selection of the convent's most important paintings. *Philip III*, *Margaret of Austria* and *Rest on the Flight into Egypt* are by Bartolomé González, court painter to Philip III. *Our Lady of the Pillar* is an 18th-century painting by the Madrid school. *St Philip* was painted by the Florentine school in the first third of the 17th century. *Margarita de Medici Portrayed as St Margaret* is a copy of the original by Justus Sustermans in the Palazzo Pitti in

Luca Giordano: St Augustine and St Monica. *Nuns' Lobby.* ▲

Florence; Margarita was the daughter of Maria Magdalena of Austria, Grand Duchess of Tuscany, who was also the sister of the convent's founder and a great patron of the arts. *St James the Moorslayer* and *St Isidore the Farmer*, both painted on stone, are 18th-century works by the Madrid school. *The Immaculate Conception* was painted by Carreño de Miranda in 1663, according to a model created specially for Vitoria Cathedral. The *Profession of Sister Ana Margarita de Austria* was a commission given by the nuns to Antonio de Pereda to mark the occasion on which Philip IV's natural daughter officially joined the convent in 1650. The canvas depicts the taking of the veil or solemn profession of the novice as laid down by the Augustinian rule. The prioress holding the black veil on Ana Margarita's right is Mariana de San José. To her left is St Augustine and at the top the

Christ Child holds a crown of roses, a symbol of religious life, with a scroll bearing the inscription: *Veni Sponsa mea et coronaveris* (Come, wife of mine and you shall be crowned). *St John the Baptist* is undoubtedly the convent's most important painting and one of the finest examples of the work of José de Ribera. It was executed in 1638 and belonged to Philip IV's collection. *The Martyrdom of St Catherine* is attributed to Marcello Venusti, whose preliminary sketch is housed in the Galleria Corsini in Rome. *Joseph's Dream* is an

Painting Room. Left, José de Ribera: St John the Baptist; *right, Bartolomé González:* Margaret of Austria. ▲

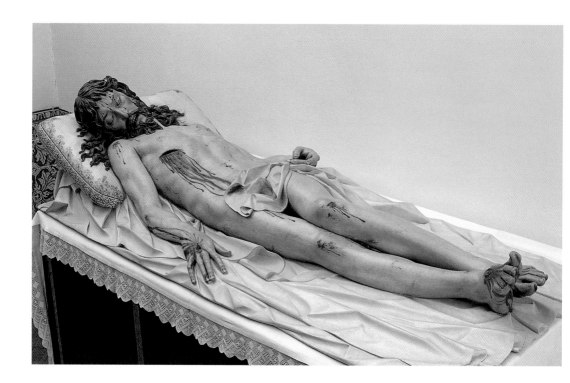

18th-century Spanish work. *The Holy Family* is Flemish panel painting by the school of Joos Van Cleve (16th century). Finally, the *Madonna and Child and Musical Angels* by the Madrid school dates from the first third of the 17th century.

The sculpture represents *Our Lady of the Kings*; it is a polychrome woodcarving crafted by Michele Perroni around 1690. The mirror is Venetian and dates from the end of the 17th century.

First floor

The Sculpture Room

This room is reached from the first landing of the Clock Staircase, which begins in the Nuns' Lobby. It has four doors: the first, mentioned previously, leads to the staircase; the door on the right leads to the Upper Cloister; the one on the left to the ante-gallery and upper gallery; and the one opposite opens into the Hall of Kings.

It contains an excellent collection of 17th-century Castilian imagery. A particularly fine example is Gregorio Fernández's *Recumbent Christ*, of which there is a replica in the Church of Santo Cristo in El Pardo. The masterful treatment of the flesh and facial expression of the figure convey with extreme realism the signs of death – the mouth gaping open, head inclined and hair soaked in sweat. The intricate pattern of the pillow is also outstanding. This sculpture presided over the Chapter House in the 17th, 18th and 19th centuries.

The *Christ at the Column*, also by Gregorio Fernández, displays the same features as the one by Pedro de Mena in the Convent of Santa Teresa de Ávila. It is notable

▲ *Gregorio Fernández:* Recumbent Christ. *Sculpture Room.*

for its pathos, the expression of pain on the face and the suffering conveyed by the blood trickling down the body, all of which are achieved by perfect carving and the use of polychrome.

The *Mater Dolorosa* was carved by José de Mora, master of Granada and royal sculptor to Charles II. It depicts with restrained naturalism the face of the Virgin and the placidity of the gesture is typical of Andalusian works of that period. De Mora may have carved this sculpture during his stay in Madrid.

According to tradition, the *ivory crucifix* dates from the time of the convent's foundation. It comprises a cross made of lignum vitae and a Hispano-Filipino polychrome ivory effigy.

Next to the *Recumbent Christ* stands an image of *Our Lady of Solitude* on a pedestal. This *alcuza* figure, specially designed to be

dressed, has a sculpted head and arms; the rest of the body consists of a large wooden frame in the shape of a truncated cone, enabling the garments to be changed easily. It is reminiscent of the 17th-century Madrid image of *Our Lady of the Dove*. From the 17th century it stood beside the Christ in the Chapter House.

The room also contains a number of paintings of the Passion of Christ: *The Head of the Saviour* is an anonymous work from Toledo; the *Descent from the Cross* is attributed to the school of Rubens; *St John, the Mater Dolorosa and Mary Magdalene* is by Felipe Diriksen and belonged to the display cabinet (now lost) that originally contained the *Recumbent Christ*; the *Ecce Homo* is a copy of the *Christ* by Titian that hangs in the Monastery of El Escorial; and the *Christ Carrying the Cross* is by Luca Giordano.

The upper gallery

Reached via the ante-gallery, the upper gallery is located at the west end of the church, at the same height as the relief of the *Annunciation* on the convent's main facade. Its three small lattice windows provide an excellent view of the church. It displays three interesting canvases: a 17th-century Flemish *Christ Carrying the Cross*; a 17th-century Spanish *Adoration of the Magi*; and an *Allegory of the Eucharist* depicting the vision of the Blessed Sacrament in the burning bush and

the hearts pierced by arrows described by the convent's founder, Mariana de San José, in her writings.

The Hall of the Kings

This room was designed to exhibit portraits of all the different members of the House of Austria who were once associated with the Royal Foundations. Except for the paintings of *Philip II, Anne of Austria, Maria Teresa of Austria, Elizabeth of Bourbon* as an adult and *Isabella Clara Eugenia*, they are all copies of works now housed in the Palazzo Pitti in Florence, which was linked to the Spanish Court through Marie de Medici (mother of Elizabeth of Bourbon) and Maria Magdalena of Austria, Grand Duchess of Tuscany, sister of Margaret of Austria and wife of Cosimo de Medici, who assembled a major collection of art at the villa Poggio Imperiale (Florence). The people portrayed in each painting are identified by inscriptions in black print that may have been added in the 19th century. In some cases the information is incorrect.

The works are described from right to left. *Margaret of Austria*, the *Cardinal Infante Ferdinand of Austria* (Philip III's son) and *Philip III* are copies of works by Bartolomé González. *Elizabeth of Bourbon*, Philip IV's first wife (Anne of Austria according to the inscription), is a copy of the original by Frans Pourbus. *Archduke Ernest*, son of the Empress Maria of Austria (the inscription identifies him as Emperor Maximilian) and *Anne of Austria*, Philip III's daughter (Empress Maria according to the inscription) are copies of paintings by Bartolomé González. *Maria Teresa of Austria, Queen of France*, daughter of Philip IV and Elizabeth of Bourbon and wife of Louis XIV, is a copy of

▲ Philip III. *Copy of an original by Bartolomé González. Hall of the Kings.*

a French painting dating from the late 17th century. *Philip II* and his fourth wife, *Anne of Austria*, are copies of works by Alonso Sánchez Coello. The original portrait of the king is now in Glasgow and that of the queen hangs in the Fundación Lázaro Galdiano in Madrid. *The Infant of Prague*, a replica of the one in the Hall of Kings at the Convent of Las Descalzas Reales, is an anonymous 17th-century work. *Our Lady of Bethlehem* is a 17th-century Spanish work. *Elizabeth of Bourbon* was painted by Rodrigo de Villadrando. *Infante Don Carlos*, *Philip IV as a Prince and Infanta Margarita*, children of

Philip II and Margaret of Austria, is a copy of a painting by Bartolomé González. *Isabella Clara Eugenia* is an original work painted by Bartolomé González in 1626. *Maria Magdalena of Austria*, Grand Duchess of Tuscany and sister of Margaret of Austria, is a copy of a work by Justus Sustermans.

The furniture in this room deserves a special mention. The Spanish leather and horsehair travelling chests with bronze nails date from the 17th century and may have arrived at the convent as part of nuns' dowries; the large pine cabinet with drawers and sliding doors is 18th-century; the two

Lower Cloister. ▲

walnut "friar's chairs" are late 17th-century Spanish pieces; and the two backless pews with lyre-shaped legs are also 17th-century Spanish. Also worthy of note are the two tables placed against the wall: one, fashioned from wood with pieces of ivory at the corners and tortoiseshell inlay, was made in Antwerp in the 17th century; the other, also of wood with inlaid ivory geometrical shapes delimited by pieces of ivory (decorated with drawings inspired by repertories of 17th-century Flemish and Italian prints) is Spanish and dates from the second half of the 18th century.

Resting on the large cabinet is a tortoiseshell and gilded bronze cross-reliquary with a beautiful ivory *Christ*, an anonymous 17th-century work. It is flanked by two 18th-century Spanish woodcarvings of the *Christ Child with Instruments of the Passion*.

Ground floor

The Lower Cloister

Returning to the Nuns' Lobby, the door opposite the convent's entrance leads to the cloister. This is one of the most important areas in the building as it is not only the hub of convent life but also its architectural backbone. Each of the walkways of this square enclosure has seven arches with large paintings set in gilded frames. The paintings are semi-circular at the top to fit the shape of the arches. They depict scenes from the life of Christ and the Virgin Mary and were given to the convent by Cardinal Antonio Zapata when his niece, María del Nacimiento, daughter of the Count and Countess of Barajas, took the habit in 1616. The hagiographer Luis Muñoz attributed them to an unspecified artist from Rome, while the

Spanish traveller and chronicler Antonio Ponz ascribed them to Vicenzo Carduccio in his *Viajes* ("Travels") published in 1772. Some researchers have attributed them to Eugenio Caxés and Bartolomé Román, though it has not yet been ascertained exactly who painted them. They were clearly produced by a number of Italian-influenced artists who may have been Italian painters established at the Madrid court, Madrid artists influenced by Italian painters or a mixture of the two.

The works are as follows: *The Immaculate Conception*, *The Birth of the Virgin*, *The Presentation of the Virgin in the Temple*, *The Annunciation*, *The Visitation of the Virgin to her Cousin St Elizabeth* and *Our Lady of O*, also called *Awaiting the Birth*, in the east walkway; *The Adoration of the Shepherds*, *The Circumcision of Christ*, *The Adoration of the Magi*, *The Purification of The Virgin*, *Jesus Among the Doctors* and *The Arrest of Christ on the Mount of Olives* on the north side; *Ecce Homo*,

The Flagellation of Christ, *Veronica Wiping the Face of Jesus* and *The Crucifixion* on the west side; and *The Resurrection*, *Noli Me Tangere*, *The Ascension*, *The Descent of the Holy Spirit*, *The Assumption of the Virgin* and *The Coronation of the Virgin* in the south walkway. Three paintings belonging to the series displayed in the west walkway are no longer extant. These are *The Descent from the Cross*, *The Entombment* and *The Women at the Sepulchre*.

Ceiling vault decorated with The Holy Spirit. *Chapel of the Lamb. Lower Cloister.* ▲

On the south side is a model of the high altarpiece fashioned by Ventura Rodríguez in 1761. It is a gilded wood niche supported by a bracket ending in a triangular pediment and is flanked by angels' heads.

In the northeast, northwest and southeast corners hang canvases painted by Van der Hamen in 1625: *St John the Baptist*, *The Martyrdom of St Sebastian*, and *The Miracle of the Crosses of St Helen*. *St Paul* is a copy made by Carlos Blanco in 1820 of a work by Van der Hamen. There is also a 19th-century copy of the Italian *Our Lady of Popolo* and a 17th-century Spanish *St Peter*. Two of the corners each have two altars covered with Talavera tiles displaying the "illustrious fleuron" design from El Escorial. Two chapels lead off from the east side of the cloister: the *Chapel of the Lamb* and the *Chapel of Our Lady of Loreto*.

The Chapel of the Lamb

This small oratory was built on the instructions of Aldonza de Zúñiga (of the Blessed Sacrament, as she was known), the convent's second prioress between 1638 and 1648.

The chapel is named after the altar painting entitled *The Apocalyptic Vision of the Lamb*, which was executed by Juan Van der Hamen in 1625.

The polychrome wooden altar was made in the 19th century and imitates 17th-century style. Its set of 17th-century Italian altar candlesticks and cross made of rock crystal and gilded bronze is particularly interesting. Also worthy of note are two 17th-century Spanish polychrome woodcarvings representing *St Agnes* and *St Margaret*.

The floor and walls are covered in Talavera tiles dating from the 17th century.

The ceiling, which was painted in tempera by artists of the Madrid school during the first third of the 17th century, depicts the *Holy Spirit Surrounded by the Fathers and Martyrs of the Early Church,* framed with polychrome gilded plant motifs.

The Chapel of Our Lady of Loreto

This chapel was commissioned by the Countess of Miranda, the mother of Aldonza de Zúñiga, who made a number of donations to La Encarnación. The main feature of this room is the polychrome wood altar with an altarpiece flanked by two pilasters with composite capitals which support a cornice adorned with two palm leaves interlaced with a floral wreath. The painting in the centre of the altarpiece is a 17th-century Spanish canvas of *Our Lady of Loreto*. The Spanish royal family was particularly devoted to this Marian image and to Our Lady Atocha, Our Lady of Good Success and Our Lady of the Miracle

The altar displays the symbol of the Virgin Mary. The two woodcarvings of *St John Nepomucen* and *St Aloysius Gonzaga* were fashioned by Luis Salvador Carmona in the 18th century and are enclosed in small 19th-century temple-shaped display cabinets. The images of *St Nicholas of Tolentino* and *St John the Evangelist* are 17th-century Spanish works. The most interesting woodcarving and one of the most important ones housed in the convent is *St John of God* by Pedro de Mena, which is notable for the saint's gaze and the asceticism he embodies. The two alabaster vases date from the late 18th century.

The vaulted ceiling was painted with tempera *candelieri* motifs by artists of the Spanish school in the first third of the 17th century. The dados of Talavera tiles date from the same century.

The antechoir

An entrance in the north walkway leads to the antechoir, a small rectangular room which in turn leads to the garden, the choir and the staircases to the refectory and cells.

The two display cabinets adorned with bronze motifs on tortoiseshell contain the wax figures of *The Ecstasy of St Teresa* and *St Anthony of Padua and the Child*, made by José de la Calleja in 1692. Between them is a 18th-century display case inlaid with ebony and ivory and surmounted with a balustrade. Inside is a Spanish polychrome woodcarving of *St John the Baptist as a Child* dating from the first quarter of the 18th century.

The room houses a number of paintings. The *Portrait of Mariana de San José Crowned with Flowers* by Francisca de Sotomayor dates from the 17th century. *The Holy Family with St John* is a copy on panel of the work by Pontormo (Jacopo Carucci) housed in the Uffizi in Florence. The *Portrait of Luisa de Carvajal* is a 17th-century Spanish painting of an interesting person. Luisa de Carvajal was a pious laywoman and a great friend of Mariana de San José who spent her estate on charitable works. She lived for a time in England, fighting against the reforms of the Anglican Church, and eventually died in London in 1614. Mariana de San José claimed her body and had it placed in the Relics Chapel at La Encarnación. The *Death Portrait of Sister Ana Margarita of Austria* was painted by an artist of the Madrid school in 1658, the year the infanta died. It shows the catafalque of Philip IV's natural daughter decorated with the flowers and candles that were customary for the wakes held for dead nuns according to the Augustinian rule. The *Purification* is an anonymous 16th-century Flemish canvas of which there is an exact copy in the Tapestry Room of the Convent of Las Descalzas Reales in Madrid. *The Descent from the Cross* is a Spanish work dating from the second half of the 17th century.

The choir

The choir, which has stood in the same spot ever since the convent was established, is only used by the community of nuns. A screen at the far end of the nuns' choir leads to the high altar of the church. A small door on the left leads to the founder's tomb and the Relics Chapel.

The Herreran-style 17th-century walnut choir stalls consist of thirty-three seats surmounted by eighteen balls; the seats are hinged and display traditional misericords

 *Gregorio Fernández: St Augustine. Choir stalls.*

with alternating volute and scallop flower motifs.

It is interesting to note the pictures of the seven archangels with their iconological attributes. They were painted by Bartolomé Román in the first third of the 17th century and depict *St Gabriel*, *St Michael*, *St Raphael*, *St Uriel*, *St Jehudiel*, *St Zadkiel* and *St Barachiel*. Above the screen is an excellent canvas by Vicenzo Carduccio, *The Holy Supper*. It was painted in 1617 for the early vaulted refectory, which is why it is shaped like a depressed arch at the top. It was valued by Roelas and Caxés in 1618, together with the church's altarpiece, and hung in pride of place in the nuns' refectory until only recently. Other paintings in this room are: *Christ at the Column*, by Bartolomé Román; *St Augustine's*

Vision of the Crucified Christ and the Virgin, by the 17th-century Madrid school; and *The Carpenter's Workshop in Nazareth*, inspired by the prints of the Wierix brothers and also painted by the Madrid school in the first third of the 17th century.

A particularly fine example of sculpture is Michele Perroni's *Recumbent Christ*, which was carved in 1690 and is enclosed in an ebony cabinet adorned with volutes and surmounted with pinnacles. Inserted in the top of the cabinet is a wooden cross with an ivory *Christ*; this figure was carved in the second half of the 17th century by Claudio Bessona, whose signature is found on the back of the loincloth.

Special mention should be also be made of Gregorio Fernández's *St Augustine* which

View of the nuns' choir towards the screen leading to the high altar of the church. ▲

stands on one of the arms of the stalls. The figure is dressed in the habit of the Augustinian Order and episcopal vestments; its left hand holds a silver church and the right a pen, symbolising St Augustine's theological writings. Opposite it is a woodcarving of *Our Lady of the Assumption*, an anonymous 17th-century Spanish work in polychrome wood.

The two 18th-century display cabinets each contain a woodcarving. One of them is *Our Lady of the Patronage*, a Spanish work dating from the second half of the 17th century. This polychrome figure, which is designed to be clothed, has jointed arms and its head is made to be fitted with a crown. Its garments and jewels are particularly rich. It is traditionally known as the "Prioress", because it is always present when novices take the veil and habit and at the demise of nuns, and occupies the prioress's place in the choir. The cult of the Patronage was introduced into Spain by Philip IV and was instituted at La Encarnación by Ana de Zúñiga (de la Concepción), prioress from 1663 to 1695. *St Joseph and the Child* also belongs to the 17th-century Spanish school, though it displays considerable Neapolitan influence.

On either side of the altar screen are two 19th-century cabinets containing woodcarvings of *St Joaquin and St Anne*, anonymous 18th-century Spanish works made of polychrome wood. The facial expression of these figures is particularly realistic and the polychrome and gilt of the clothing is painstakingly done. They were previously located in a room called the "Corito" or "little choir", which has a circular window or oeil-de-boeuf that gives onto one of the sides of the high altar of the church through which the nuns' choir screen is visible. This window can be seen from the high altar.

To the right of the screen is the tomb of Sister Ana Margarita of Austria (who is portrayed in pictures in the Painting Room and antechoir). It is built in black marble and

veined amber and surmounted by a carved and gilded wooden coat of arms of the House of Austria, supported by two angels. It dates from 1672.

It is interesting to note that the nuns' cemetery is located beneath the choir and that nuns have been buried there since the convent was founded. Only people who

The room also contains a 17th-century Mexican cane paste *Christ*, two small panel paintings depicting *The Face of the Virgin* and King Abgar's *The Holy Face of Christ*. The latter, painted by the 18th-century Spanish school, reproduces an acheropita (acheiropoietos) type image [not made by human hand]. The three images traditionally regarded as being of this kind are this one, Veronica's Veil and the Holy Shroud. Above the lintel of the door leading to the Relics Chapel is a plaster model of the *Church of St John Lateran* in Rome. It is flanked by two niches containing plaster images of *St John* and *St Peter*. All three date from the 18th century.

The Relics Chapel

This is the most important room in the convent and one of the most exceptional relics chapels of all the Spanish royal foundations. It was built at the same time as the convent as a response to the House of Austria's wish to establish sacred areas to house relics retrieved from holy places and from European countries undergoing Lutheran reform. It has received relics in their corresponding reliquaries since 1616, though the richest items – as regards both quantity and artistic quality – date from the 17th and 18th centuries.

The room is located behind the high altar in the church and its walls are fitted with a number of display cabinets resting on bracket-shaped supports. Each of the cabinets comprises two sections: a lower part, divided into several compartments with hinged glass doors; and an upper part consisting of two rows of small compartments with glass panels screwed into the wood. On the projecting cornice on top of each cabinet are **bust-reliquaries** in polychrome carved wood

played a significant role in the convent for various reasons are interred in special places close to the high altar, such as in the choir or the Relics Chapel. Such is the case of Ana Margarita de Austria, Mariana de San José and Luisa de Carvajal.

Mother Mariana

To the left of the screen a door leads to the room containing the tomb of the convent's founder, Mariana de San José. This small room is located between the nuns' choir and the Relics Chapel. The rectangular tomb, which stands on a base surrounded by moulding, is made of wood and has a truncated pyramid-shaped lid. It is painted in a manner that imitates red and black marble and was crafted in the second half of the 19th century.

▲ Reliquary of St Pantaleon *with the flask containing his blood. Relics Chapel.*

which date from the first half of the 17th century. The 17th-century dado is made of patterned Talavera tiles displaying the El Escorial "illustrious fleuron" motif.

The room has three doors: the one to the right of the altar leads to the room containing Mariana de San José's tomb; the one to the left of the altar leads to the priests' sacristy; and the one opposite it leads to the kitchen garden.

The altar of the Relics Chapel stands behind the church tabernacle and the monstrance is positioned at exactly the same height as it. The altarpiece is made of gilded wood and is surmounted by a semicircular pediment. At the centre is a panel painting of *The Nativity* by Bernardino Luini (c. 1525), a follower of Leonardo; on the back of the painting – and therefore not normally visible – is *The Lamb*. The altar is surrounded by small

cabinets with gilded bronze ornamentation containing gilded bronze reliquaries in the shape of small temples.

On the altar is the gilded bronze and rock crystal *monstrance* which was given to the convent by the Marchioness of Zahara when her daughter Teresa de Jesús took her vows in 1619. It consists of a temple within a temple. The inner, octagonal one rests on eight bronze lions supporting a stepped pedestal from which eight crystal barley-sugar columns with gilded silver pedestals and capitals rise. Resting on the capitals, an entablature adorned with palmettes and cherubs supports a glass dome engraved with vegetal motifs. The outer temple is square and has a semicircular arch at each corner flanked by fluted columns resting on pedestals. It is surmounted by a groined vault resting on a drum with large consoles and oval glass panels.

Ceiling of Relics Chapel. Vicenzo Carducci. ▲

On either side of the monstrance two woodcarvings attributed to Salzillo depict saints venerated by the Augustinian Order: *Our Lady of Solace* and *St Augustine*.

The ceiling was embellished by Carducci, though some historians maintain that Bayeu made some additions to it in the 18th century when the church was remodelled. At the centre is a large oval showing the *Trinity* surrounded by angels. Around it are a number of smaller ovals containing paintings of six early Christian martyrs: Agnes, Catherine, Cecilia, Ursula, Barbara and Margaret. Grotesques and *candelieri* motifs complete the ceiling decoration.

The Relics Chapel houses seven hundred items. These include reliquaries, oil paintings on copper, polychrome wood, ivory and alabaster carvings, medals and rosaries, to name a few.

The reliquaries can be classified into different types. One is the **small chests or caskets** of different sizes and materials – ebony, tortoiseshell, silver and ivory. Particularly interesting examples are: the 18th-century tortoiseshell and silver chests from Mexico; the 17th-century namban; and the 17th-century ebony, silver and ivory chests which are part of the Maundy Thursday monument.

The reliquaries in the form of **small temples** are made of gilded bronze. The relics are enclosed in a geometrically shaped glass container that rests on a support or shaft with mouldings. The most important

▲ Epiphany *reliquary. Ebony, bronze, silver and oil on copper. Anonymous Italian work, first half of 17th century. Relics Chapel.*

example – not only of this type but of all the reliquaries housed in this room – is the *reliquary of St Pantaleon*. According to tradition, Pantaleon's blood, contained in a small flask, liquefies in the church every year on the 27th of July.

The **ostensory-type reliquaries** date from the 17th and 18th centuries. These reliquaries consist of an ebony frame decorated with inlaid semiprecious stones and gilded bronze that holds an oval or quadrangular piece into which is inserted an oil painting on agate or copper surmounted by a pediment. They have a number of cavities containing relics. These paintings on agate and copper, like the octagonal oil paintings on copper, were undoubtedly intended originally for private oratories (even though they later came to be housed in public institutions) and were probably diplomatic gifts or presents sent to the religious institutions by members of the European courts. The paintings are anonymous and are inspired by Italian works of the second half of the 16th century which are known from repertories of prints. They are probably Florentine.

Another type, most of the examples of which date from the 17th century, consists of **niches**. These reliquaries resemble altarpieces or architectural facades and contain a gilt bronze or ivory sculpture in the round. They are also Italian.

The cardboard and wood **panels** in the upper sections of the cabinets are interesting examples of craftsmanship. They are lined in silk and display bones, sewn in place,

surrounded by beads and passementerie. These items were made by the nuns during the 19th and 20th centuries.

Also worthy of mention are the **pyramid-shaped** ebony and gilded bronze reliquaries which came from the Netherlands in the 17th century, as well as the carved, polychrome wood **reliquaries in the shape of a hand or arm**. These also contain relics of saints.

By the door leading to the kitchen garden is the wooden chest containing the body of Luisa de Carvajal.

Finally, other items in the room include: 17th-century **sets of coral** altar crosses and candlesticks from Palermo; an ivory *St Sebastian* tied to a column, made in southern Germany in the 17th century; an excellent wax Theatine Nativity scene made by the Neapolitan Ermenegildo Sicili in about 1777; an 18th-century *Christ Child with Instruments of the Passion* set of polychrome woodcarvings; and the small polychrome woodcarving of an *Ecce Homo* by Pedro de Mena.

The Priests' Sacristy

This room is used by priests to prepare for services held in the church. It is connected to the Nuns' Sacristy by means of a revolving window in one of the corners through which the nuns' chief sacristan passes the liturgical ornaments and silver vessels to be used during the service. The painting of *The Parable of the Marriage Feast*, executed by Bartolomé Román in 1638, bears witness to the clothing worn and the type of tableware and kitchen utensils used at the time. Other canvases are: *St James* and *St John the Evangelist*, attributed to Antonio del Castillo; *St Anne and the Virgin and Child*, a

▲ *Top, Vicenzo Carducci;* St Philip; *bottom, Gregorio Ferro:* St Augustine and the Mystery of the Holy Trinity. *Church of La Encarnación.*

View of the church nave. ▶

17th-century Spanish work; and a *Christ Risen* by Vincenzo Carducci.

Above the door to the Relics Chapel hangs a gilded wood cabinet decorated with scrollwork and volutes. It contains an 18th-century ivory *crucifix* mounted on a gilded wood base.

The two flat-topped walnut chests of drawers with panelled drawers and iron handles are Spanish and date from the 17th century. On one of the chests stands a 17th-century ebony *crucifix-reliquary* with a gilt bronze effigy.

The ante-sacristy

A door opposite the picture by Bartolomé Román in the Priests' Sacristy leads to the ante-sacristy. Walnut benches adorned with rectangular panels and surmounted by three Escorial-type balls run along the right-hand side of this room. On the left are two walnut chests with panelled drawers and iron handles; they are surmounted by a wooden panel, also with Escorial-type balls. A small staircase between them leads to the high altar.

The walls display paintings by the Madrid school of the first third of the 17th century based on the Wierix brothers' prints: *The Birth of the Virgin*, two scenes depicting *The Holy House of Nazareth* and *The Embrace before the Golden Gate*, and a *Penitent Magdalen* and *St Agnes*, also 17th-century Spanish works.

The two woodcarvings in the room represent: *Our Lady of Hope*, the patron saint of the brotherhood of the same name which was founded in 1734 and no longer exists; and a *St Ildephonsus* belonging to the brotherhood of the Hijosdalgo, the feast of whose patron saint, St Alfonso, is celebrated in the convent on 23rd January.

The church

The church of the Convent of La Encarnación is one of the most beautiful

and important in Madrid. It was fully refurbished by Ventura Rodríguez according to Juan Gómez de Mora's original layout.

The *Life of the Venerable Mariana de San José*, written by Luis Muñoz in 1646, describes the interior of the convent and original church. Muñoz mentions the seven altars, each with a

Antonio González Velázquez: St Augustine Before the Holy Trinity. *F. Gutiérrez and I. Carnicero, stuccowork. Church vault.* ▲

canvas by Vicenzo Carducci, and four balconies: two on the Gospel side used by the monarchs and musicians; and two on the Epistle side, one of which was used by important personages and the other for the organ sent to the convent by Isabella Clara Eugenia from the Netherlands. The current organ dates form the 19th century and has undergone a number of alterations. It has been restored and is used both for liturgical celebrations and for organised concerts.

The church's present structure dates from 1761-1763 when the prioress, Ana María de la Aurura (daughter of the Count and Countess of Bornos) and the senior chaplain, Vicente Pignatelli, commissioned the architect Ventura Rodríguez to remodel the church. The works were funded by the two thousand gold doubloons bequeathed by the queen, Barbara of Bragança, in her will. The prioress considered that the old altarpieces were in a very poor state of repair and had a new one made from Tortosa marble.

The church's ground plan is a Latin cross. The transepts hardly project from the nave and the presbytery is separated from the crossing by six marble steps. Only the choir screen to the right of the high altar and the doors on either transept are visible. The right-hand door leads to the **forecourt in Calle Encarnación**, and the one on the left, now sealed, once opened onto the corner of the west side of the lower cloister.

The canvases on the high altar and two side altars came from old altarpiece and were painted by Vincenzo Carducci in 1616. The painting in the centre depicts *The Annunciation*; the one above the left-hand altar depicts *St Philip* and the one on the right *St Margaret*, in memory of the convent's founders. The canvases which hang in the nave were painted by 18th-century Madrid artists. On the left are *St Augustine and the Mystery of the Holy Trinity* by Gregorio Ferro and *St Augustine Giving Alms to the Poor* painted by José de Castillo around 1785 from a preparatory sketch housed in the Museo de Bellas Artes in Santander. To the right are *St Augustine Against the Donatists*, by Ginés de Aguirre, and *The Death of St Augustine* by Francisco Ramos. The frescoes in the nave were painted by Luis González Velázquez and depict *St Ambrose, The Baptism of St Augustine* and *The Sacrifice of Manoah*. On the pendentives are *The Guardian Angel, St Michael, St Gabriel* and *St Raphael*, while the two frescoes above the crossing show the four remaining archangels – *Jehudiel, Uriel, Zadkiel* and *Barachiel* – painted by the González Velázquez brothers. The fresco on the dome was painted by Antonio González Velázquez and depicts *St Augustine Before the Holy Trinity*. Finally, the fresco over the presbytery showing *The Apparition of the Crucified Christ and the Virgin Mary to St Augustine* was painted by Francisco Bayeu. The sketch is housed in the drawings section of the Museo del Prado.

On either side of the high altarpiece are polychrome woodcarvings of *St Augustine* and *St Monica*, also from the original church and painted by Juan Muñoz, a follower of Gregorio Fernández. The *angels* above the St Philip altar were made by Juan Pascual de Mena and the *angels* above the St Margaret altar by Felipe Castro. On the side where the St Philip altar stands is an image of *St Pantaleon* fashioned by Font of Olot.

The tabernacle on the high altar, made of jasper, marble and gilded bronze, was designed by the master architect. Of particular interest is the door, which has a bas-relief of *The Saviour* by silversmith Domingo Urquiza.

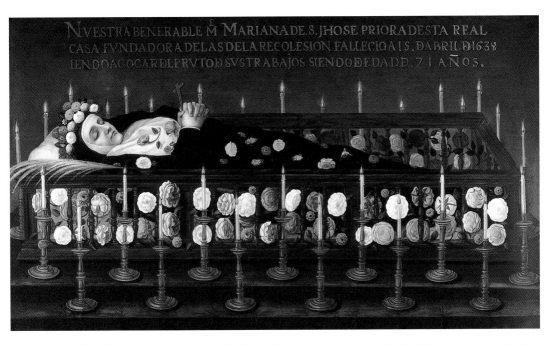

NVESTRA BENERABLE M̃ MARIANA DE.S.JHOSE PRIORA DESTA REAL
CASA FVNDADORA DE LAS DELA RECOLESION FALLECIOA IS. DABRIL DI638
IENDOAGOCARDLERVTODSVSTRABAJOS SIENDODEDADD. 7 I AÑOS.

Top, Upper Cloister. Bottom, Death portrait of Mother Mariana de San José, *1638. Spanish school. Chapel of St Augustine.* ▲

All three tabernacles were designed by Isidro Carnicero.

Juan González was responsible for the architectural design of the church. Francisco Gutiérrez worked on the stuccowork frieze of the dome; Isidro Carnicero on the stuccowork around the window and crossing; Antonio Primo on the medallions on each of the two side galleries; and Manuel Arévalo Pacheco on the royal coats of arms on the west side of the crossing.

The enclosure

VARIOUS INTERESTING works are not included in the tour. However, they have at some time been shown in temporary exhibitions or addressed in studies such as monographs and doctoral theses, and the collections of liturgical ornaments and silver altar vessels are used daily in religious ceremonies. In order to provide clear information on the most important pieces housed within the enclosed area, they are discussed in the context of the collections to which they belong rather than according to their location (as with the Museum), as most of the convent's inner rooms are areas where the nuns go about their daily affairs and are not of particular artistic interest.

Paintings

The most important collection of paintings in this area consists of twenty-five canvases depicting the early Christian martyrs. Located in the **Upper Cloister**, they were painted by artists of the Madrid School in the first third of the 17th century. The series was inspired by the frescoes painted by Nicola Circignani (known as Pomerancio) for the church of San

Stefano Rotondo in Rome in 1583. They were a gift to the convent from the founder, Philip III, and have remained in the same room ever since. The name of each martyred saint is shown in Latin in a cartouche at the bottom of each painting. They are as follows: *St Vitalis, The Maccabbees, St Ursula, St Agapitus, St Lucy, St Agatha, St Blandina, St Calixtus, St John Ante Portam Latinam, St Ignatius of Antioch, St Polycarp, St Cecilia, St Apollonia, St Vincent, SS Cyprian and Justina, St Perpetua, SS Erasmus and Blaise, SS Jacob, John, Paul and Barbara, The Martyrs of the severed hands, St Denys, St Stephen, St Agnes, SS Gervase and Protase, SS Cosmas and Damian* and *St Catherine*.

The Upper Cloister stands exactly above the Lower Cloister but is not as high; the parapets are built in the manner of iron balconies and the walls which display the canvases of the martyrs form semicircular arcades like those on the lower floor. Following the layout of the Chapel of the Lamb and the Chapel of Our Lady of Loreto, two small oratories also lead off from the Upper Cloister: the Chapel of Christ, where Gregorio Fernández's *Recumbent Christ* (now in the Sculpture Room) was originally housed, and St Joseph's Chapel, which takes its name from a 19th-century stucco carving of *St Joseph and the Child*.

Other works of interest include two canvases painted in 1658 and 1678 by Pedro Ruiz González. The first depicts *The Glorification of St Thomas Aquinas*, and the second represents *The Apparition of the Virgin to St Philip Neri* (both in the Nuns' Sacristy). The painting of *Philip IV* is attributed to Pedro Villafranca (second parlour) and shows the convent's second patron with all the characteristics of a court portrait. *The Apparition of Christ to the Ailing St Vincent Ferrer* is by José García Hidalgo (second

parlour). The *Mater Dolorosa* was painted by Miguel Herrera in 1782 (study).

The Augustinian Martyrs of Japan paintings are by José María Romero (there are three versions, two in the archives corridor and one in the second parlour). The *Portrait of Father Gabino* is a tribute to one of the visitors to the convent who made a supreme effort to prevent disentailment being enforced in the convent in the 19th century (first parlour). *St Pantaleon* is also worthy of mention due to

the devotion to this saint at the convent and locally.

The following works are Spanish and date from the 17th century: *St Nicholas of Tolentino* (St Augustine's Chapel); the *Death Portrait of Mother Mariana de San José*, which was painted in 1638 and displays the same iconographic features as the portrait of Sister Ana Margarita de Austria lying on her catafalque (St Augustine's Chapel); *The Christ of Patience* (refectory); *Vision of the Glory* (refectory);

Left, The Good Shepherd Seated on the Fountain of Life. *Polychrome ivory. Goa, 17th century. Right, Gregorio Fernández:* ▲
The Immaculate Conception. *Chapel of the Immaculate Conception. Enclosure.*

87

St Clare of Montefalco (infirmary); *The Transit of the Virgin* (archives corridor); *The Guardian Angel of the Community,* a work by Bartolomé Román based on the seven archangels of the choir with medallions representing scenes from the life of Mariana de San José in each corner (main dormitory corridor); the *Portrait of Sister Ana Margarita de Austria* in an Augustinian habit and the Contemptus Mundi in her hand (second parlour); and a *Flight into Egypt* (study).

There are also a number of copies of works by other painters: *The Mystic Marriage of St Catherine* is a copy of the original by Correggio (St Augustine's Chapel); *The Holy Family with SS Elizabeth and John* is a copy of the original by Scipione Pulzone (archives corridor); *St Anne Teaching the Virgin to Read* is a copy of the original by Rubens (doctor's surgery); *St Sebastian* is a copy of a work by Titian (archives corridor); *The Annunciation* is a copy of a painting by Vicenzo Carducci (outside the main dormitory); and *The Guardian Angel of the Community* is a copy of Gaspar Becerra's painting in the Guardian Angel Chapel at the Convent of Las Descalzas Reales (Chapel of Christ).

Sculpture

The sculptures housed in the enclosed area can be divided into the following categories: **Virgins**, **crucifixes**, **saints** and **Christ child** images. One of the most important Marian images is an *Immaculate Conception* by Gregorio Fernández which stands in the chapel of the same name. It is enclosed in a carved and gilded wood altar niche with a semicircular arch resting on pilasters and Corinthian columns. The sculpture is one of the artist's earliest works – possibly executed before 1620 – and was a gift to the community

from the countess of Nieva; it originally stood in a chapel of its own in the Upper Cloister. One of the convent's most cherished pieces is undoubtedly the polychrome wood miniature of *Our Lady of Peace with the Child*, a Spanish work of the first third of the 17th century. Located in the large kitchen, it rests on an 18th-century baldachin of polychrome carved wood. Devotion to Our Lady of Peace is deeply rooted among the nuns of La Encarnación, as this image accompanied Mariana de San José to all the Augustinian convents she founded – which is why it is also known as "The Founder". The third and last Virgin is located in the Novices' Room: a woodcarving designed to be dressed representing *Our Lady as a Girl*, executed by the Spanish school in the first half of the 17th century. Like other images of this kind, only the face and hands are sculpted. The image, which has a wig, stands in a wood and

Pedro Roldán: St Augustine, 17th century. Polychrome woodcarving. Chapel of St Augustine. Upper Cloister. Enclosure. ▲

tortoiseshell temple-shaped cabinet fashioned by Spanish craftsmen around 1645. This cabinet consists of a base of alternating straight and curved lines, a semicircular recess flanked by two gilt bronze barley-sugar columns and an entablature of the same shape as the base surmounted with two angels, also made of gilt bronze. On the roof, above a small gilt bronze niche, is a polychrome ivory sculpture in the round representing *The Good Shepherd* seated on the Fountain of Life, carved in Goa in the first half of the 17th century.

One of the Convent of La Encarnación's finest collections is its ivory **crucifixes**. Although the most interesting items are on display in the Museum, mention should be made of three located in different rooms in the enclosure. The first one, in the Chapel of the Immaculate Conception, is an exquisitely made 17th-century Italian *reliquary of Christ* nailed to an ebony cross with gilt bronze ornamentation; the cross is enclosed in a pedestal-reliquary with five compartments. This piece is kept in a 17th-century Spanish ebony display cabinet with a slightly mounded top and bottom. The second crucifix presides over the refectory. A small ivory Christ with silver reinforcements on the cross, it may have been made by a follower of Alonso Cano in the second half of the 17th century. Finally, a magnificent 17th-century *Hispano-Philippine effigy* stands on the 19th-century altar in the nuns' infirmary; the cross is made of rosewood with ivory inlay and gilded bronze reinforcements.

Some of the most interesting woodcarvings of **saints** are located in St Augustine's Chapel, which is presided over by an image of the saint after which it is named. This image is one of the most interesting examples of Augustinian

Nuns' Sacristy. Left, Damián de Castro: Alms chalice of Charles IV, 1779-82; ▲ *right, Lesmes del Moral and J. Carranza: Alms chalice of Ferdinand VII, 1822.*

iconography in the convent and also of Castilian imagery of that period. A superb polychrome wood carving fashioned by Pedro Roldán in the last third of the 17th century, it stands inside a carved gilt wood altar niche crafted by the woodcarver Raimundo Duarte in the second half of the 19th century. The 19th-century display cabinets at the far end of the chapel contain two 17th-century Spanish polychrome woodcarvings: *St Thomas of Villanueva*, an Augustinian saint, richly attired in his bishop's cope and mitre and holding a crozier; and *St Stephen*, dressed in a deacon's dalmatic with a medallion alluding to strength and stones associated with his martyrdom.

To end the section on sculpture, mention should be made of a number of interesting iconographic representations of the **Christ child**. Some rooms in the Museum contain figures of the Christ child with instruments of the Passion, images of the Christ child enthroned such as *The Emmanuel* (popularly known as "Manolitos") and images of the Christ child and the Virgin in glory, showing Jesus bearing the sceptre, crown and globe of the world. The images most frequently used for the nuns' celebrations are located in the enclosure. Particularly fine examples are *The Little Lost Child*, *The Little Prisoner* and *The Child with the Grapes*. *The Little Lost Child* is a small late 17th-century polychrome ivory carving fashioned in Portuguese India in the late 17th century. It is used in the game of hide-and-seek played by the nuns on the feast day of the Holy Family (the prioress hides the image and the nun who finds it can choose any Christ child and keep it for a whole day). *The Little Prisoner* is a late 18th-century Spanish woodcarving of the Christ child seated on a rock in the manner of a throne adorned with fruit, trees and

seashells; the blazing heart is a reference to the growing dedication to the cult of the Sacred Heart. Finally, *The Child with the Grapes*, a late 18th-century Spanish polychrome woodcarving, shows the Christ child seated on the globe of the world eating grapes as a symbol of Jesus as the true saviour and the true vine.

Silverwork and gold

The nuns' Sacristy houses 82 silver altar vessels – chalices, ciboria, chrism vessels, candlesticks, wafer boxes – of which the so-called "alms chalices" are particularly noteworthy. These items were fashioned especially for the king, who presented them as an offering during the Epiphany (6th January) Eucharist in remembrance of the gifts made by the Three Kings to the newborn Jesus. Subsequently the king's chief almsgiver (hence the name of the chalices) delivered them to the Royal Foundations or to poor parishes. The Convent of La Encarnación possesses two superb examples: one of chiselled and repoussé gilded silver made for Charles IV by the Cordovan silversmith Damián de Castro between 1779 and 1782; the other one of chiselled and enamelled gilded silver, was made for Ferdinand VII by Lesmes del Moral and Juan Carranza in 1822.

Liturgical cloths

The convent's collection of 942 liturgical cloths is kept in the Nuns' Sacristy. Subject to the liturgical regulations dictated by the Church over the centuries, they are used regularly and may therefore be said to form a "living" collection. As a result of the changes in liturgical legislation, particularly

in the wake of the Second Vatican Council, many items are no longer used owing to their shape (guitar-shaped chasubles), to the abolition of certain vestments (maniples, amices) or to the prohibition of certain colours (black). Some of the most important sets of vestments are kept in the chests of drawers in the Nuns' Sacristy, which, like those in the Priests' Sacristy, are made of walnut with panelled drawers and iron handles. They are Spanish and date from the 17th century. The *Set of Vestments of the Skulls* is made of brocade with a black background embroidered in gold with Renaissance motifs – flowers and volutes – framing the skulls. It was made in Spain in the 17th century and was obviously worn during funeral services. The *Gold and Red Set of Vestments*, also known as that of the founder, Margaret of Austria, was fashioned in Europe, possibly Germany,

around 1600. It consists of a number of red velvet vestments embroidered with geometric and plant motifs. The so-called 18th-century *bizarre silks* display fantasy motifs inspired by nature. Finally, the *Tomb Cloth* of the Spanish monarchs, made in Spain during the reign of Charles III, was placed over royal catafalques supporting coffins. It is a large square of black velvet with appliqués in several colours forming volutes and leaves. Also in appliqué work are the royal coats of arms of Charles III and María Amalia of Saxony in the centre and skulls at the corners. It is bordered with a yellow fringe.

Tomb Cloth of the Spanish monarchs. Rule of Charles III. Nuns' Sacristy. Enclosure. ▲

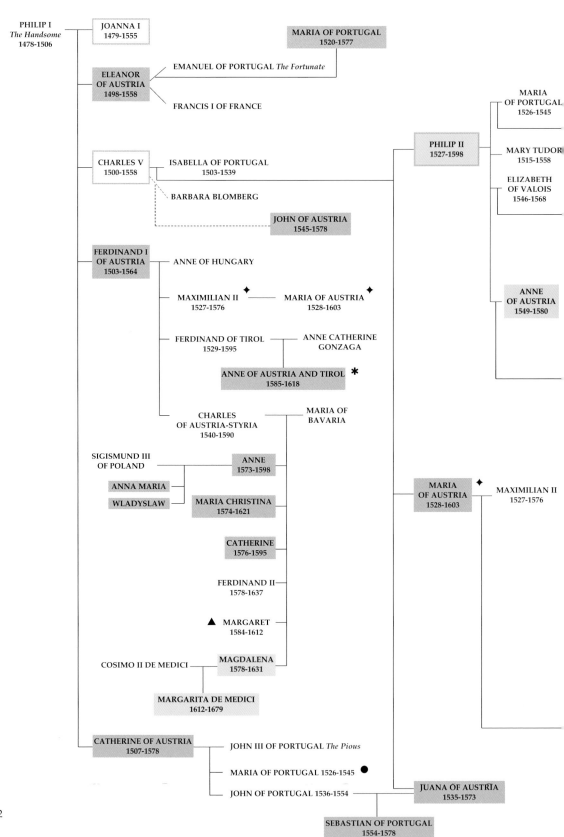

PHILIP I
The Handsome
1478-1506

JOANNA I
1479-1555

MARIA OF PORTUGAL
1520-1577

ELEANOR
OF AUSTRIA
1498-1558

EMANUEL OF PORTUGAL *The Fortunate*

FRANCIS I OF FRANCE

MARIA
OF PORTUGAL
1526-1545

PHILIP II
1527-1598

MARY TUDOR
1515-1558

CHARLES V
1500-1558

ISABELLA OF PORTUGAL
1503-1539

ELIZABETH
OF VALOIS
1546-1568

BARBARA BLOMBERG

JOHN OF AUSTRIA
1545-1578

FERDINAND I
OF AUSTRIA
1503-1564

ANNE OF HUNGARY

ANNE
OF AUSTRIA
1549-1580

MAXIMILIAN II
1527-1576

MARIA OF AUSTRIA
1528-1603

FERDINAND OF TIROL
1529-1595

ANNE CATHERINE
GONZAGA

ANNE OF AUSTRIA AND TIROL *
1585-1618

CHARLES
OF AUSTRIA-STYRIA
1540-1590

MARIA OF
BAVARIA

SIGISMUND III
OF POLAND

ANNE
1573-1598

MARIA
OF AUSTRIA
1528-1603

MAXIMILIAN II
1527-1576

ANNA MARIA

WLADYSLAW

MARIA CHRISTINA
1574-1621

CATHERINE
1576-1595

FERDINAND II
1578-1637

▲ MARGARET
1584-1612

COSIMO II DE MEDICI

MAGDALENA
1578-1631

MARGARITA DE MEDICI
1612-1679

CATHERINE OF AUSTRIA
1507-1578

JOHN III OF PORTUGAL *The Pious*

MARIA OF PORTUGAL 1526-1545 ●

JOHN OF PORTUGAL 1536-1554

JUANA OF AUSTRIA
1535-1573

SEBASTIAN OF PORTUGAL
1554-1578

SYNTHESIS OF THE GENEALOGICAL TREE OF THE HOUSE OF AUSTRIA
Personages connected with the convents of Las Descalzas Reales and La Encarnación

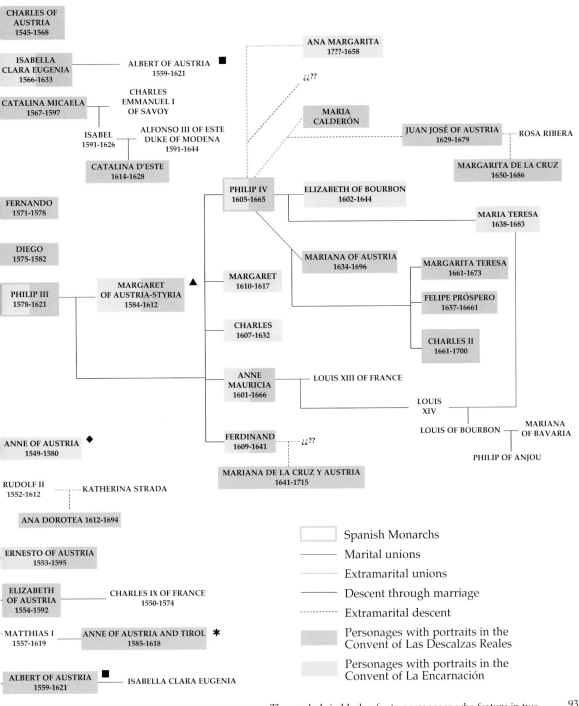

CHARLES OF AUSTRIA 1545-1568

ISABELLA CLARA EUGENIA 1566-1633 — ALBERT OF AUSTRIA 1559-1621 ■

ANA MARGARITA 1???-1658

CATALINA MICAELA 1567-1597 — CHARLES EMMANUEL I OF SAVOY

¿¿??

MARIA CALDERÓN

ISABEL 1591-1626 — ALFONSO III OF ESTE DUKE OF MODENA 1591-1644

JUAN JOSÉ OF AUSTRIA 1629-1679 ---- ROSA RIBERA

CATALINA D'ESTE 1614-1628

MARGARITA DE LA CRUZ 1650-1686

FERNANDO 1571-1578

PHILIP IV 1605-1665 — ELIZABETH OF BOURBON 1602-1644

MARIA TERESA 1638-1683

DIEGO 1575-1582

MARIANA OF AUSTRIA 1634-1696

MARGARITA TERESA 1661-1673

PHILIP III 1578-1621 — MARGARET OF AUSTRIA-STYRIA 1584-1612 ▲ — MARGARET 1610-1617

FELIPE PRÓSPERO 1657-16661

CHARLES 1607-1632

CHARLES II 1661-1700

ANNE MAURICIA 1601-1666 — LOUIS XIII OF FRANCE

LOUIS XIV

ANNE OF AUSTRIA 1549-1580 ◆

FERDINAND 1609-1641 ---- ¿¿??

LOUIS OF BOURBON — MARIANA OF BAVARIA

PHILIP OF ANJOU

MARIANA DE LA CRUZ Y AUSTRIA 1641-1715

RUDOLF II 1552-1612 ---- KATHERINA STRADA

ANA DOROTEA 1612-1694

ERNESTO OF AUSTRIA 1553-1595

ELIZABETH OF AUSTRIA 1554-1592 — CHARLES IX OF FRANCE 1550-1574

MATTHIAS I 1557-1619 — ANNE OF AUSTRIA AND TIROL 1585-1618 ✱

ALBERT OF AUSTRIA 1559-1621 ■ — ISABELLA CLARA EUGENIA

INFANTA MARGARITA 1567-1633

Spanish Monarchs

—— Marital unions

······ Extramarital unions

—— Descent through marriage

······ Extramarital descent

Personages with portraits in the Convent of Las Descalzas Reales

Personages with portraits in the Convent of La Encarnación

The symbols in black refer to personages who feature in two different places.

93

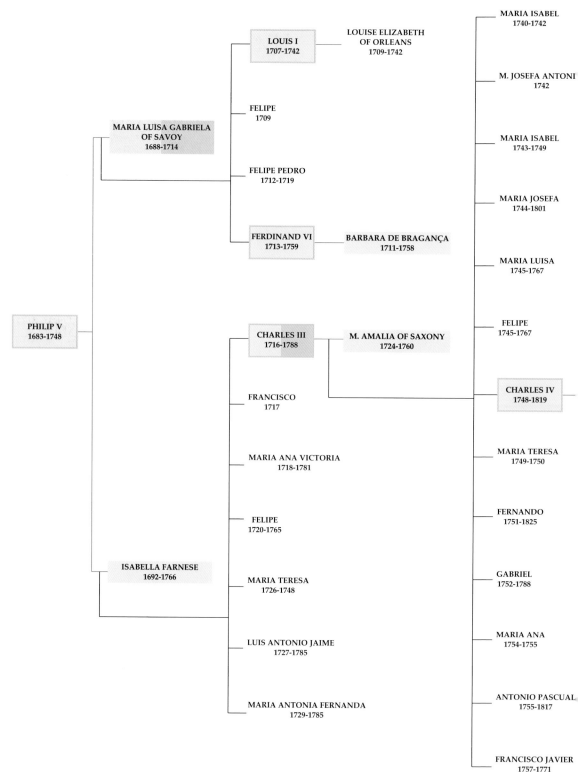

PHILIP V
1683-1748

MARIA LUISA GABRIELA
OF SAVOY
1688-1714

LOUIS I
1707-1742

LOUISE ELIZABETH
OF ORLEANS
1709-1742

FELIPE
1709

FELIPE PEDRO
1712-1719

FERDINAND VI
1713-1759

BARBARA DE BRAGANÇA
1711-1758

ISABELLA FARNESE
1692-1766

CHARLES III
1716-1788

M. AMALIA OF SAXONY
1724-1760

FRANCISCO
1717

MARIA ANA VICTORIA
1718-1781

FELIPE
1720-1765

MARIA TERESA
1726-1748

LUIS ANTONIO JAIME
1727-1785

MARIA ANTONIA FERNANDA
1729-1785

MARIA ISABEL
1740-1742

M. JOSEFA ANTONI
1742

MARIA ISABEL
1743-1749

MARIA JOSEFA
1744-1801

MARIA LUISA
1745-1767

FELIPE
1745-1767

CHARLES IV
1748-1819

MARIA TERESA
1749-1750

FERNANDO
1751-1825

GABRIEL
1752-1788

MARIA ANA
1754-1755

ANTONIO PASCUAL
1755-1817

FRANCISCO JAVIER
1757-1771

SYNTHESIS OF THE GENEALOGICAL TREE OF THE SPANISH BOURBONS
Personages connected with the convents of Las Descalzas Reales and La Encarnación

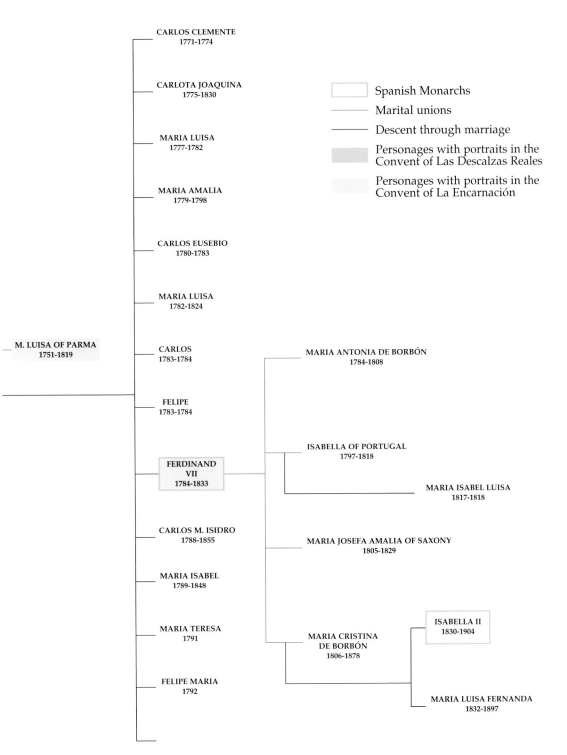

CARLOS CLEMENTE
1771-1774

CARLOTA JOAQUINA
1775-1830

MARIA LUISA
1777-1782

MARIA AMALIA
1779-1798

CARLOS EUSEBIO
1780-1783

MARIA LUISA
1782-1824

M. LUISA OF PARMA
1751-1819

CARLOS
1783-1784

MARIA ANTONIA DE BORBÓN
1784-1808

FELIPE
1783-1784

ISABELLA OF PORTUGAL
1797-1818

FERDINAND
VII
1784-1833

MARIA ISABEL LUISA
1817-1818

CARLOS M. ISIDRO
1788-1855

MARIA JOSEFA AMALIA OF SAXONY
1805-1829

MARIA ISABEL
1789-1848

MARIA TERESA
1791

ISABELLA II
1830-1904

MARIA CRISTINA
DE BORBÓN
1806-1878

FELIPE MARIA
1792

MARIA LUISA FERNANDA
1832-1897

Spanish Monarchs

Marital unions

Descent through marriage

Personages with portraits in the
Convent of Las Descalzas Reales

Personages with portraits in the
Convent of La Encarnación

General Bibliography

ALVÁREZ BAENA, J.A.: *Compendio histórico de las grandezas de la coronada villa de Madrid, corte de la monarquía de España*. Madrid, 1786.

ANGULO ÍÑIGUEZ, D. and PÉREZ SÁNCHEZ, A. E.: *Historia de la pintura española: la escuela madrileña del primer tercio del siglo XVII*. Madrid, 1969.

Antonio de Pereda (1611-1678) y la pintura madrileña de su tiempo. Madrid, 1978.

BARBEITO CARNEIRO, Mª I.: *Escritoras madrileñas del siglo XVII (estudio bibliográfico crítico)*. Madrid, 1986.

BERMEJO, E.: "Primitivos flamencos 1. Pintura IX. Colecciones del Patrimonio Nacional", *Reales Sitios*, 33 (1972); 34 (1972); 35 (1973).

BONET CORREA, A.: *Los Monasterios Reales del Patrimonio Nacional*. Madrid, 1984.

BONET CORREA, A.: *Iglesias madrileñas del siglo XVII*. Madrid, 1984.

BORDAS, C.: *Instrumentos musicales. Colecciones españolas*. Madrid, 2001. Vol. II.

En torno a la mesa: Tres siglos de formas y objetos en los palacios y monasteries reales. Madrid, 2000.

El Corazón de España. Alexandria-Louisiana, 2003.

Felipe II, un monarca y su época. La monarquía hispánica. San Lorenzo de El Escorial, 1998.

GARCÍA SANZ, A.: "Relicarios de Oriente", *Oriente en Palacio. Tesoros asiáticos en las colecciones reales españolas*. Madrid, 2003.

GARCÍA SANZ, A. and SÁNCHEZ HERNÁNDEZ, Mª L.: "Monasterios reales españoles: iconografía de monjas, santas y beatas", *Consejo Superior de Investigaciones Científicas, VIII Jornadas de Arte*, Madrid, 1997.

GARCÍA SANZ, A. and SÁNCHEZ HERNÁNDEZ, Mª L.: *Las Descalzas y la Encarnación (Dos clausuras de Madrid)*. Madrid, Patrimonio Nacional, 1999.

Juan Gómez de Mora (1586-1648) arquitecto y trazador del rey y maestro mayor de obras de la villa de Madrid. Madrid, 1986.

JUNQUERA, P.: "Belenes monásticos del Patrimonio Nacional", *Reales Sitios*, 18 (1968).

La ilusión de la belleza. Una geografía de la estética. Valencia, 2001.

Las clausuras madrileñas: el ciclo de Navidad. Madrid, 1996.

LOZOYA, Marqués de: "Antonio de Pereda en el Patrimonio Nacional y en los Patronatos Reales", *Reales Sitios*, 7 (1966).

MARTÍN GARCÍA, F.: *Catálogo de la plata del Patrimonio Nacional*. Madrid, 1987.

MARTÍN GARCÍA, F.: "Piezas de la platería hispanoamericana en el Patrimonio Nacional", *Reales Sitios*, 112 (1992).

MARTÍN GARCÍA, F.: *L'Art de l'argenteria a les Colleccions Reials*. Palma de Mallorca, 1995.

MARTÍN GARCÍA, F.: *Joyas de la orfebrería del Patrimonio Nacional*. Seville, 1995.

MARTÍN GARCÍA, F.: *El arte de la platería en las Colecciones Reales*. Salamanca, 1996.

MARTÍN GARCÍA, F.: *El arte de la platería en las Colecciones Reales*. Oviedo, 1997.

Navidad en Palacio: Reales Sitios, Monasterios y Salzillo. Madrid, 1998.

Navidad en Palacio: Belenes Napolitanos. Madrid, 1999.

Navidad en Palacio: de Nazaret a Belén. Madrid, 2002.

Oriente en Palacio. Tesoros asiáticos en las colecciones reales. Madrid, 2003.

PÉREZ PASTOR, C.: *Noticias y documentos relativos a la historia y literature españolas*. Madrid, 1914. Vol. II.

QUINTANA, J. de la: *A la muy antigua, noble y coronada villa de Madrid: historia de sus antiguedad, nobleza y grandeza*. Madrid, 1639.

RUIZ ALCÓN, Mª T.: "La Anunciación en la pintura de los Palacios y Fundaciones Reales", *Reales Sitios*, 18 (1968).

RUIZ ALCÓN, Mª T.: "Lucas Jordán", *Reales Sitios*, 28 (1971); 29 (1971); 30 (1971); 31 (1972); 32 (1972).

RUIZ ALCÓN, Mª T.: "Pintura sobre piedra en el Patrimonio Nacional", *Reales Sitios*, 38 (1973).

RUIZ ALCÓN, Mª T.: "Los arcángeles en los monasterios de Las Descalzas Reales y de la Encarnación", *Reales Sitios*, 40 (1974).

RUIZ ALCÓN, Mª T.: "Obras de restauración en el monasterio de Las Descalzas Reales y de la Encarnación de Madrid, realizadas por técnicos del Patrimonio Nacional", *Reales Sitios*, 87 (1986).

SAINZ DE ROBLES, F.C.: *Historia y estampas de la villa de Madrid*. Madrid, 1932.

SÁNCHEZ HERNÁNDEZ, Mª L.: "Fundaciones Reales madrileñas: génesis, evolución y proyección", *Madrid en el contexto de lo hispánico. Universidad Complutense*, 1992.

SÁNCHEZ HERNÁNDEZ, Mª L.: *Patronato Regio y órdenes religiosas femeninas en el Madrid de los Austrias. Descalzas Reales, Encarnación y Santa Isabel*. Madrid, 1997.

SANCHO, J.L.: *La arquitectura de los Sitios Reales. Catálogo Histórico de los Palacios, Jardines y Patronatos Reales del Patrimonio Nacional*. Madrid, 1995.

SIMÓN DIAZ, J.: "Los monasterios de Las Descalzas Reales y de la Encarnación", *Villa de Madrid*, 66 (1980-1981).

TORMO Y MONZÓ, E.: *Las iglesias del antiguo Madrid*. Madrid, 1927.

TOVAR MARTÍN, V.: *Arquitectura madrileña del siglo XVII. Datos para su estudio*. Madrid, 1983.

Bibliography on Las Descalzas Reales

Alonso Sánchez Coello y el retrato en la Corte de Felipe II. Madrid, 1990.

ANDRADA, R.: "Restauraciones y nuevas obras: Descalzas Reales", *Reales Sitios*, 22 (1969).

ANTONIO SAENZ, T.: "Sobre unas obras de Diego de Urbina en el Monasterio de Las Descalzas Reales de Madrid", *Consejo Superior de Investigaciones Científicas, III Jornadas de Arte*. Madrid, 1991.

BARRIO MOYA, J.L.: "La iglesia de Las Descalzas Reales de Madrid según un inventario de 1703", *Anales del Instituto de Estudios Madrileños*, XXXIV (1994).

CADIÑANOS BARDECI, I.: "Dos encargos para la iglesia de Las Descalzas Reales", *Archivo Español de Arte*, 263 (1993).

CARRILLO, Fray J. de: *Relación histórica de la Real Fundación del Monasterio de Las Descalzas de Santa Clara de la villa de Madrid.* Madrid, 1616.

CEÑAL, R.: *Viaje de la emperatriz María de Austria a España. Con estancia prolongada en Las Descalzas Reales. Reales Sitios,* 75 (1983).

CHECA CREMADES, F.: "Monasterio de Las Descalzas Reales: orígenes de su colección artística", *Reales Sitios,* 112 (1989).

"El 'Fray Angélico' en Las Descalzas Reales", *Reales Sitios,* 27 (1990).

ESTELLA, M.: "Artistas madrileños en el Palacio del Tesoro (Descalzas Reales), en el Palacio de Pastrana y otros monumentos de interés", *Archivo Español de Arte,* 229 (1985).

"Exposición en Milán de figuras del Niño Jesús", *Reales Sitios,* 102 (1989).

FABRE, F.: "El altar mayor de Las Descalzas Reales", *Semanario Pintoresco Español,* 1839.

FERNÁNDEZ RETANA, L.: "Doña Juana de Austria, 1535-1573", Madrid, 1955.

Fundación Carlos de Amberes. Madrid, 1989.

GARCÍA SANZ, A.: "El pastorcillo. Imagen del Niño Jesús en el Monasterio de Las Descalzas Reales". Belén, No. 21 (2002).

GARCÍA SANZ, A.: "El Nacimiento Napolitano del Monasterio de Las Descalzas Reales de Madrid". Belén, No 16 (2000).

GARCÍA SANZ, A.: "Devoción del Niño Jesús del Santo Pesebre. Escultura relicario de Las Descalzas Reales". Belén, No. 17 (2000).

GARCÍA SANZ, A.: "Nuevos datos sobre los artífices de la capilla funeraria de Juana de Austria", *Reales Sitios,* 155 (2003).

GARCÍA SANZ, A.: "Una 'Oración en el huerto' sobre el sepulcro de la emperatriz María", Reales Sitios, 113 (1992).

GARCÍA SANZ, A. and MARTÍNEZ CUESTA, J.: "La serie iconográfica de ermitaños del monasterio de Las Descalzas Reales", *Coloquios de Iconografía,* Madrid, 1990.

GARCÍA SANZ, A. and RUDOLF, K. F.: "Mujeres coleccionistas de la Casa de Austria en el siglo XVI", *Consejo Superior de Investigaciones Científicas, VIII Jornadas de Arte,* Madrid, 1997.

GARCÍA SANZ, A. and RUIZ, L.: "Linaje regio y monacal. La galería de retratos de Las Descalzas Reales", Linaje del Emperador. Cáceres, 2002.

GARCÍA SANZ, A. and TRIVIÑO, Mª V.: *Iconografía de Santa Clara en el Monasterio de Las Descalzas Reales.* Madrid, 1993.

GARCÍA SANZ, A.: "Nuevas aproximaciones a la serie El Triunfo de la Eucaristía", *El Arte en la Corte de los Archiduques Alberto de Austria e Isabel Clara Eugenia (1598-1633). Un reino imaginado,* 1999.

GARCÍA SANZ, A. and JORDAN GSCHWEND, A.: "Via Orientalis: Objetos del lejano oriente en el Monasterio de Las Descalzas Reales", *Reales Sitios,* 138 (1998).

Gonzalez Asenjo, E.: "Dionisio Mantuano y la "Casita de Nazaret", *Reales Sitios,* 140 (1999).

GUERRA DE LA VEGA, R.: "Velázquez y las esculturas del Patrimonio Nacional", *Reales Sitios,* 27 (1990).

HEBAS, J. de las: *Historia breve de la portentosa imagen de Nuestra Señora del Milagro, que se venera e el religiosísimo convento de las Señoras descalzas Reales de esta Corte.* Madrid, 1793.

JORDÁN GSCHWEND, A.: "Los retratos de Juana de Austria posteriores a 1554: La imagen de una Princesa de Portugal, una Regente de España y una jesuita", *Reales Sitios*, 151 (2002).

JUNQUERA, P.: "Descalzas Reales: Capilla del Milagro", *Reales Sitios*, 22 (1969).

JUNQUERA, P.: "Las Descalzas Reales a la vez convento y museo", *Goya*, 42 (1961).

JUNQUERA, P.: "Las nuevas instalaciones de tapices en el Palacio Nacional y Las Descalzas Reales", *Archivo Español de Arte*, 173 (1971).

JUNQUERA, P.: "Monasterio de Las Descalzas Reales", *Reales Sitios*, supplement (1969).

JUNQUERA, P. and JUNQUERA, J.J.: "La Apoteosis de la Eucaristía. Descalzas Reales. Serie de Tapices", *Reales Sitios*, 22 (1969).

LOPEZ DE HOYOS, J.: *Hystoria y relación verdadera de la enfermedad felicissimo tránsito y sumptuosas exequias fúnebres de la Sereníssima Reyna de España doña Isabel de Valoys nuestra señora.* Madrid, 1569.

LOZOYA, Marqués de: "Ampliación del museo de Las Descalzas Reales", *Reales Sitios*, 22 (1969).

LOZOYA, Marqués de: "El convento de Las Descalzas Reales abierto al público como museo", *Archivo Español de Arte*, 134 (1961).

Niños Jesús. *Sculture policrome dalle Collezioni Reali di Madrid.* Milan, 1989.

MATILLA TASCÓN, A.: "Restauración de obras de arte en Las Descalzas Reales. Siglos XVII y XVIII", *Revista de Archivos, Bibliotecas y Museos*, 76 (1973).

MESONERO ROMANOS, R. de: "Iglesia de Las Descalzas Reales", *La Ilustración Española y Americana*, 8th April (1903).

MUÑOZ GONZÁLEZ, Mª J.: "Dionisio Mantuano y la Casita de Nazaret", *Reales Sitios*, 140 (1999).

OLIVERAS GUART, A.: "Amplias restauraciones en la clausura de Las Descalzas Reales", *Reales Sitios*, 23 (1970).

ORTEGA VIDAL, J.: "La Capilla sepulcral de Doña Juana en Las Descalzas Reales. Una joya en la penumbra", *Reales Sitios*, 138 (1998).

PALMA, J. de la: *Vida de la serenísima infanta sor Margarita de la Cruz.* Madrid, 1636.

PÉREZ DE GUZMAN, J.: "Descalzas Reales de Madrid. Capilla interior de Nuestra Señora del Milagro", *La Ilustración Española y Americana*, 30th January (1912).

PORTÚS, J.: "Las Descalzas Reales en la cultura festiva del barroco", *Reales Sitios*, 138 (1998).

RODRÍGUEZ G. DE CEBALLOS, A.: "Arte y mentalidad religiosa en el Museo de Las Descalzas Reales", *Reales Sitios*, 138 (1998).

ROMERO COLOMA, A. M.: "El Ecce Homo y la Dolorosa de Pedro de Mena en el Monasterio de Las Descalzas Reales", *Reales Sitios*, 126 (1995).

ROMERO COLOMA, A. M.: "Estudio iconográfico y estético de la Dolorosa de José Risueño", *Reales Sitios*, 130 (1996).

ROSELL Y TORRES, I.: "El retablo de Las Descalzas Reales", *Museo Español de Antigüedades*, V (1895).

Ruiz Alcón, Mª T.: "Arquetas relicarios de Las Descalzas Reales", *Reales Sitios*, 45 (1975).

Ruiz Alcón, Mª T.: "Descalzas Reales: Capilla de la Dormición y Casita de Nazaret", *Reales Sitios*, 22 (1969).

Ruiz Alcón, Mª T.: "El cuadro de Santa Úrsula y las once mil vírgenes de Las Descalzas Reales de Madrid", *Archivo Español de Arte*, 258 (1992).

Ruiz Alcón, Mª T.: "Imágenes del Niño Jesús del monasterio convento de Las Descalzas Reales", *Reales Sitios*, 6 (1965).

Ruiz Alcón, Mª T.: *Monasterio de Las Descalzas Reales*. Madrid, 1987.

Ruiz Alcón, Mª T.: "Santa Teresa en los monasterios de el Escorial y de Las Descalzas Reales", *Reales Sitios*, 74 (1982).

Ruiz Gómez, L.: "Marcantonio Raimondi y La última cena de Las Descalzas Reales de Madrid", *Lecturas de Historia del Arte*, Vitoria, 1994.

Ruiz Gómez, L.: *La colección de estampas devocionales de Las Descalzas Reales*. Madrid, 1998.

Ruiz Gómez, L.: "Dos nuevos lienzos de la escuela madrileña en Las Descalzas Reales de Madrid, y una hipótesis sobre la devoción al Santo Sepulcro", *Reales Sitios*, 138 (1998).

Salazar, Fray P. de: *Crónica y historia de la fundación y progreso de la Provincia de Castilla, de la Orden del bienaventurado padre San Francisco. Dirigido a la serenissima señora doña Margarita de Austria y de la Cruz*. Madrid, 1612.

Sánchez Cantón, F. J.: "¿Quién fue el pintor Georgius que firma un retrato en Las Descalzas Reales?", *Archivo Español de Arte*, 62 (1944).

Souto, J. L.: "Esculturas de Pedro de Mena en Budia (Guadalajara). Una Dolorosa y un Ecce-Homo, réplica de otro de Las Descalzas Reales", *Reales Sitios*, 75 (1983).

Toajas Roger, Mª A.: "Arquitectura del Monasterio de Las Descalzas Reales. La capilla de San José", *Anales de Historia del Arte*, 8 (1998).

Toajas Roger, Mª A.: "Juana de Austria y las artes", *Felipe II y las artes*, Madrid, 2002.

Toajas Roger, Mª A.: "Memoria de un Palacio madrileño del siglo XVI: Las Descalzas Reales", *Reales Sitios*, 142 (1999).

Tormo y Monzó, E.: *En Las Descalzas Reales. Estudios históricos, iconográficos y artísticos*. Madrid, 1917.

Tormo y Monzó, E.: *Treinta y tres retratos en Las Descalzas Reales: estudios históricos, iconográficos y artísticos*. Madrid, 1934.

Tormo y Monzó, E.: *En Las Descalzas Reales de Madrid: Los Tapices. La Apoteosis Eucarística de Rubens*. Madrid, 1945.

Tormo y Monzó, E.: *En Las Descalzas Reales de Madrid. Estudios históricos, iconográficos y artísticos*. Madrid; 1947.

Wethey, H. and Sunderland Wethey, A.: "Herrera Barnuevo y su capilla de Las Descalzas Reales", *Reales Sitios*, 13 (1967).

Zunzunegui, J. A.: "La archiduquesa Isabel Clara Eugenia y los tapices de Las Descalzas Reales", *Vértice*, 29 (1940).

Bibliography on La Encarnación

Agulló and Cobo, M.: "Noticia de algunos artistas que trabajaron en el real monasterio

de la Encarnación", *Villa de Madrid*,
42 (1973).

Angulo, D. and Pérez Sánchez, A.:
"Pintura madrileña", *Reales Sitios*, 73 (1983).

Antonio Saénz, T. de: "Nuevos datos para el
estudio del monasterio de la Encarnación",
Anales del Instituto de Estudios Madrileños,
XXIV (1987).

Aterido Fernández, A.: "Una nueva obra de José
de Churriguera: el monumento de semana santa
del monasterio de la Encarnación", *Anales del
Instituto de Estudios Madrileños*, T. XXXV (1995).

Ayape, E.: *La sangre de San Pantaleón en Madrid*.
Madrid, 1987.

Balao González, A.: "La restauración de
Iuseppe Ribera en el Patrimonio Nacional",
Reales Sitios, 114 (1992).

Barbeito Carneiro, I.: "Aproximación
bibliográfica a la madre Mariana de
San José, una fundadora de excepción",
Recollectio, 9 (1986).

*Barroco Español y Austríaco: fiesta y teatro en la
corte*. Madrid, 1994.

Bedat, C.: *El escultor Felipe de Castro*.
Santiago de Compostela, 1971.

Bustamante García, A.: *Los artífices del real
convento de la Encarnación*. Valladolid, 1975.

Capdepón, P.: *La música en el monasterio de la
Encarnación. Siglo XVIII*. Madrid, 1997.

Catálogo-Exposición Gregorio Fernández, Madrid,
1999.

*El emporio de Sevilla. Cuarto centenario de la
construcción de la Real Audiencia*. Seville, 1995.

El linaje del Emperador. Cáceres, 2000.

Esparraguera Calvo, G. and Verdaguer
Martín, M. A.: "El monasterio de la
Encarnación: la desamortización e intervención
del arquitecto Narciso Pascual y Colomer".
Villa de Madrid, 85 (1985).

García de Armesto, J.: *Guía histórico descriptiva
de la real capilla y monasterio de la Encarnación de
esta corte*. Madrid, 1916.

González Palacios, A.: *Las Colecciones Reales
españolas de mosaicos y piedras duras*.
Museo del Prado, 2001.

Junquera, P.: "Escultura del monasterio de la
Encarnación", *Reales Sitios*, 4 (1965).

Junquera, P.: "Santiago en la pintura y
escultura del Patrimonio Nacional",
Reales Sitios, 28 (1971).

Kawamura, Yayoi: "Obras de laca del arte
'namban' en los monasterios de la Encarnación
y de las trinitarias de Madrid", *Reales Sitios*,
147 (2001).

*La morte e la gloria. Apparati funebri medicei per
Filippo II di Spagna e Margherita d'Austria*.
Florence, 1999.

López Serrano, M.: "El monasterio de la
Encarnación", *Reales Sitios*, 4 (1965).

Lozoya, Marqués de: "El real monasterio de la
Encarnación, un nuevo museo en Madrid",
Goya, 376 (1964).

Luca Giordano y España. Madrid, 2002.

Marqués del Saltillo: "El real monasterio de
la Encarnación y artistas que allí trabajaron
(1614-1621)", *Revista de la biblioteca, archivo y
museo del Ayuntamiento de Madrid*, 50 (1944).

MARTÍN GARCÍA, F.: "Cálices limosneros. Capilla de palacio y monasterio de la Encarnación y de El Escorial", *Reales Sitios*, 62 (1979).

MUÑOZ, L.: *Vida de la venerable madre Mariana de San José*. Madrid, 1646.

NELTING, D.: "Nicolo Circignanis Fresken in Santo Stefano Rotondo und Antonio Gallonios *Tratatto de gli istrumenti de martirio*", Band, 113 (2001).

PÉREZ SÁNCHEZ, A.: Carreño. Avilés, 1985.

PINILLOS IGLESIAS, Mª N.: *Hilando oro. Vida de Luisa de Carvajal*. Madrid, 2001.

Ribera: 1595-1652, Madrid, 1992.

RUIZ ALCÓN, Mª T.: *Guía del real monasterio de la Encarnación*. Madrid, 1978.

RUIZ MANERO, J. M.: "Obras y noticias de Girolamo Muziano, Marcello Venusti y Scipione Pulzone en España", *Archivo Español de Arte*, 272 (1995).

RUIZ MANERO, J. M.: "Pintura italiana del siglo XVI en España: Leonardo y los leonardescos", *Cuadernos de Arte e Iconografía*, V, 9, 1992.

SÁNCHEZ HERNÁNDEZ, Mª L.: *El monasterio de la Encarnación de Madrid: un modelo de vida religiosa en el siglo XVII*. Salamanca, 1986.

SÁNCHEZ HERNÁNDEZ, Mª L.: "El monasterio de la Encarnación: una fundación real en el siglo XVII", *Reales Sitios*, 89 (1986).

SÁNCHEZ HERNÁNDEZ, Mª L.: "Un manuscrito de Santa Teresa en el monasterio de la Encarnación de Madrid", *Reales Sitios*, 101 (1989).

SÁNCHEZ HERNÁNDEZ, Mª L.: *Mariana de San José: vida y obra de una monja en el siglo XVII*

(Dissertation for Theology degree. Instituto Superior de Pastoral, Universidad Pontificia de Salamanca, 1998).

SÁNCHEZ HERNÁNDEZ, Mª L.: "El Belén del monasterio de la Encarnación de Madrid", Belén, 1999.

SÁNCHEZ HERNÁNDEZ, Mª L.: "El Niño Jesús de Praga", Belén, September 2001.

SÁNCHEZ HERNÁNDEZ, Mª L.: "Iconografía agustiniana en el Monasterio de la Encarnación de Madrid", La Ciudad de Dios, Monasterio de El Escorial, 2003.

Santiago la esperanza. Xacobeo 99. Xunta de Galicia, 1999.

TORMO, E.: "Visitando lo no visitable. La clausura de la Encarnación", *Boletín de la sociedad española de excursiones*, XXV (1917).

TORMO, E.: "Apéndice a la clausura de la Encarnación", *Boletín de la sociedad Española de Excursiones*, XXV, 1917.

TORRÓN, F.: "Cristo yacente de Gregorio Fernández en el monasterio de la Encarnación", *Reales Sitios*, 114 (1992).

URREA, J.: "Un boceto de José del Castillo en el Museo de Santander", *Universidad de Valladolid, Seminario de Arte y Arqueología*, 1983.

Ventura Rodríguez: *Exposición conmemorativa*. Madrid, 1983.

THIS BOOK, PUBLISHED BY PATRIMONIO NACIONAL,
WAS PRINTED ON 7 OCTOBER 2003, FEAST DAY OF OUR LADY OF THE ROSARY,
AT ESTUDIOS GRÁFICOS EUROPEOS IN MADRID.